BIG WHITE FOG

Theodore Ward

Other Titles in this Series

Theodore Ward

BIG WHITE FOG

NICK HERN BOOKS

London

www.nickhernbooks.co.uk

A Nick Hern Book

Big White Fog first published in Great Britain as
a paperback original in 2007 by Nick Hern Books Limited,
14 Larden Road, London W3 7ST

*Every effort has been made to trace all copyright holders.
The publishers will be pleased to receive information about
any omissions and make the necessary arrangements at the
first opportunity.*

Cover image: 'Strike Captain during protest by the packing
house workers, Chicago, 1948' by Wayne F. Miller

Cover design: Ned Hoste, 2H

Typeset by Country Setting, Kingsdown, Kent CT14 8ES
Printed and bound in Great Britain by Biddles, King's Lynn

A CIP catalogue record for this book is available from
the British Library

ISBN 978 1 85459 595 9

Contents

Theodore Ward

James Theodore (Ted) Ward was born on 15 September 1902 to John and Louise Ward in Thibodaux Louisiana, forty miles west of New Orleans. He was the sixth of eleven children. His father was born into slavery, and became a devoutly religious schoolmaster who sold patent medicines and books to supplement his income.

While still a young boy, Ted wrote a small play and showed it to his father who proclaimed it to be 'the work of the devil' and threw it on the fire. When Ted was twelve his mother died, the family broke up and he ran away from home. He rode the freight trains north, and travelled extensively, working variously as a bell-hop, shoe-shine boy, and barber-shop porter. He finally ended up in Salt Lake City, Utah, where he was briefly jailed, began to write again, and attended the University of Utah. He entered a story in a magazine contest, winning first prize. As a result, a Utah newspaper editor, Gale Martin, encouraged him to apply for a Zona Gale creative-writing scholarship which he won, allowing him to attend the University of Wisconsin from 1931–33 where he hosted a radio show and gained a reputation for his dramatic readings.

Having moved to Chicago in 1934, he wrote a one-act play called *Sick 'n' Tiahd*, which was produced in 1937 and won him second prize in a drama contest sponsored by the Chicago Repertoire Group; the winner was Richard Wright, who encouraged him to join the South Side Writers Workshop and to write a full-length play. This play became *Big White Fog*, completed in 1937 and produced by the Negro Unit of the Chicago Federal Theatre Project (FTP) in 1938.

Ward then wrote several more plays: *Even the Dead Arise*, *The Falcon of Adawa*, *Skin Deep* and an adaptation of Richard Wright's short story *Bright and Morning Star*. In 1939 he came to New York in the chorus of the FTP's *The Swing Mikado*.

In 1940 he joined Langston Hughes, Paul Robeson, Theodore Browne, Richard Wright and Alain Locke in forming the Negro Playwrights Company based in New York City. Their

first production was a revival of *Big White Fog* at the Lincoln
Theatre in Harlem. Also in 1940, he married Mary Sangigian,
an Armenian-American social activist. They had two
daughters, Laura and Elise, and were married for twenty-three
years. Mrs Ward died in 2007 aged 95.

In 1947, Ward's historical drama *Our Lan'* was produced off-
Broadway at the Grand Street Playhouse, transferring to
Broadway's Royale Theatre and winning him the Theatre
Guild Award. That same year he was named Negro of the Year
by the Schomberg Collection of the New York Public Library.
Ward was later a recipient of the John Simon Guggenheim and
National Theatre fellowships for playwriting.

Further plays include *Shout Hallelujah!*, *John Brown*, *Of
Human Grandeur*, *Madison*, *John de Conquerer*, *Candle in the
Wind*, *Whole Hog or Nothin'*, *Charity*, *Throwback*, *The
Daubers*, *The Bell and The Light*, and *Big Money*. Ted Ward
was also a renowned and respected poet.

During the 1940s and '50s, Ted Ward struggled to make a
living solely as a writer. During World War II, he contributed
to the war effort by writing news and broadcasting scripts for
the Office of War Information. With the 1953 appointment of
Senator Joseph McCarthy as Chair of the House Un-American
Activities Committee, Ward's career as a progressive writer,
like those of so many artists and intellectuals, was almost
completely suppressed until the re-emergence in the 1960s of
black theatre, black nationalism, and a rediscovery by younger
black dramatists of his work and his outspoken voice.

Ward returned to Chicago in 1963 to head the Louis Theatre
and School of Drama at the South Side Centre for the
Performing Arts. During the 1970s he was playwright in
residence for a year at the University of Massachusetts and for
several seasons at the New Orleans Free Southern Theatre.

In 1977 in recognition of his many accomplishments,
contributions, and prestigious awards, the Mayor of Chicago
declared 23 April of that year as Theodore Ward Day. In 1985,
Columbia College, Chicago, established the Theodore Ward
Prize for African American Playwriting, awarded annually to
emerging and established black playwrights.

Theodore Ward died on 8 May 1983.

Power, Knowledge and Dignity (1920)

Marcus Garvey

There is now a world of revival of thought and action, which is causing people everywhere to bestir themselves towards their own security, through which we hear the cry of 'Ireland for the Irish, Palestine for the Jew, Egypt of the Egyptian, Asia for the Asiatics' and thus we Negroes raise the cry of 'Africa for the Africans', those at home and those abroad.

Some people are not disposed to give us credit for having feelings, passions, ambitions and desires like other races; they are satisfied to relegate us to the back-heap of human aspirations; but this is a mistake. The Almighty Creator made us men, not unlike others, but in His own image; hence, as a race, we feel that we, too, are entitled to the rights that are common to humanity . . .

All men should be free – free to work out their own salvation. Free to create their own destinies. Free to nationally build up themselves for the upbringing and rearing of a culture and civilization of their own. Jewish culture is different from Irish culture. Anglo-Saxon culture is unlike Teutonic culture. Asiatic culture differs greatly from European culture; and, in the same way, the world should be liberal enough to allow the Negro latitude to develop a culture of his own. Why should the Negro be lost among other races and nations of the world and to himself? Did nature not make him a son of the soil? Did the Creator not fashion him out of the dust of the earth? Out of that rich soil to which he bears such a wonderful resemblance? A resemblance that changes not, even though the ages have flown? No, the Ethiopian cannot change his skin; and so we appeal to the conscience of the white world to yield us a place of national freedom among the creatures of the present-day temporal materialism . . .

We believe in justice and human love. If our rights are to be respected, then, we, too, must respect the rights of all mankind; hence, we are ever ready and willing to yield to the white man the things that are his, and we feel that he, too, when his conscience is touched, will yield to us the things that are ours.

We should like to see a peaceful, prosperous and progressive white race in America and Europe; a peaceful, prosperous and progressive yellow race in Asia, and, in like manner, we want, and we demand, a peaceful, prosperous and progressive black race in Africa. Is that asking too much? Surely not. Humanity, without any immediate human hope of racial oneness, has drifted apart, and is now divided into separate and distinct groups, each with its own ideals and aspirations. Thus, we cannot expect any one race to hold a monopoly of creation and be able to keep the rest satisfied.

From a speech delivered to an audience of 25,000 at Madison Square Garden, New York City, on 1 August 1920.

Enter the New Negro (1925)

Alain Locke

The Negro, for his part, has idols of the tribe to smash. If on the one hand the white man has erred in making the Negro appear to be that which would excuse or extenuate his treatment of him, the Negro, in turn, has too often unnecessarily excused himself because of the way he has been treated. The intelligent Negro of today is resolved not to make discrimination an extenuation for his shortcomings in performance, individual or collective; he is trying to hold himself at par, neither inflated by sentimental allowances nor depreciated by current social discounts. For this he must know himself and be known for precisely what he is, and for that reason he welcomes the new scientific rather than the old sentimental interest . . .

The fiction is that the life of the races is separate, and increasingly so. The fact is that they have touched too closely at the unfavourable and too lightly at the favourable levels . . .

With the American Negro, his new internationalism is primarily an effort to recapture contact with the scattered peoples of African derivation. Garveyism may be a transient, if spectacular phenomenon, but the possible role of the American Negro in the future development of Africa is one of the most constructive and universally helpful missions that any modern people can lay claim to.

From Enter the New Negro *by Alain Locke.*

Published in Survey Graphic: Harlem, Mecca of the New Negro, *March 1925. © Survey Associates Inc.*

Our Conception of Theatre and its Function (1940)

Theodore Ward

I once encountered a statement which had been written by one
Julius Bob, for one of the encyclopedias, and which I believe
is representative of the Negro Playwrights Company's idea of
the theatre it hopes to build here in Harlem. 'Every theatre,' he
said, 'in the true sense of the word is a unity, at the core of
which is the living community finding some vital part of itself
reflected in the creations of dramatist and actor.'

We must get the people to see it is an error to assume that
some discrepancy obtains between a vital theatre and a theatre
of amusement.

Perhaps, as among all oppressed peoples, large sections of our
group *are* given to looking upon the theatre primarily as a means
of escape. But the theatre was not a means of escape in its
inception and it has never been such, so far as we are aware, at
any highpoint in its history. The idea that it was designed to
give light amusement is but one of the current falsehoods which
have been concocted by those who are contemptuous of the
intelligence of the common man, and who would have others
believe that he lacks the wit to understand what is serious, or
the vision to determine for himself what is entertaining and
good. It is the product of those who wish to keep the people in
ignorance, so that they may be more easily exploited. It is the
lie of those who label everything as propaganda that does not
conform to their own interests and opinion. It is but a subtle
part of the technique which has culminated in the current attacks
upon Civil Liberties here, and the burnings, abroad, of books;
the hounding of the Jewish people, the flagrant dissemination
of the lies of racism, and the destruction of democracy . . .

Being Negroes ourselves, we are convinced that our people
want to be rid of fear, and scepticism, of the gloom and despair
encouraged in some quarters as the natural accompaniment of
the lot of victims of oppression . . .

We know that Harlem can possess such a theatre that reflects
all the grace and the beauty and the historical truth of our daily
life, a theatre that gives voice to the best that men have thought
and believed; that boldly and honestly deals with the major
problems of the world, and that depends on the deepest interest

and aspirations of the race for its dignity and inspiration.
Surely there can be no drama more compelling, more vital,
more exciting, more interesting, more all-engrossing than that
which manifests a coming to grips with life without evasion
and affirms with candour the warm aspirations of a people who
have come of age and demand their immediate freedom!

From a speech given on the occasion of the Negro Playwrights
Company's Benefit at the Golden Gate Ballroom, Harlem,
New York City, 6 September 1940.

Death on the City Pavements (1941)

Richard Wright

The trains and the autos move north, ever north, and from
1916 to 1928 1,200,000 of us were moving from the south to
the north and we kept leaving . . .

We see white men and women get on the train, dressed in
expensive new clothes. We look at them guardedly and wonder
will they bother us. Will they ask us to stand up while they sit
down?: will they tell us to go to the back of the coach? Even
though we have been told that we need not be afraid, we have
lived so long in fear of all white faces that we cannot help but
sit and wait. We look around the train and we do not see the
old familiar signs: FOR COLORED and FOR WHITE. The
train speeds north and we cannot sleep. Our heads sink in a
doze, and then we sit bolt-upright, prodded by the thought that
we must watch these strange surroundings. But nothing
happens; these white men seem impersonal and their very
neutrality reassures us – for a while. Almost against our deeper
judgement, we try to force ourselves to relax, for these brisk
men give no sign of what they feel. They are indifferent. O
sweet and welcome *indifference*! . . .

There are so many people . . . The apartments in which we
sleep are crowded and noisy and soon enough we learn that the
brisk, clipped men of the North, the Bosses of the Buildings,
are not at all *indifferent* . . . No longer do our lives depend on
the soil, the sun, the rain, or the wind; we live by the grace of
job and the brutal logic of jobs . . .

The Bosses of the Buildings take these old houses and convert
them into 'kitchenettes', and then rent them to us at rates so

high they make fabulous fortunes before the houses are too old for habitation . . .

Sometimes five or six of us live in a one-room kitchenette, a place where simple folk such as we should never be held captive . . .

The kitchenette scatters death so widely among us that our death rate exceeds our birth rate, and if it were not for the trains and autos bringing us daily into the city from the plantations, we black folks who dwell in northern cities would die out entirely over the course of a few years . . .

The engineering, aviation, mechanical, and chemical schools close their doors to our sons, just as the great corporations which make thousands of commodities refuse to employ them. The Bosses of the Buildings decree that we must be maids, porters, janitors, cooks, and general servants . . .

Having been warned against us by the Bosses of the Buildings, having heard tall tales about us, about how 'bad' we are, white people react emotionally as though we had the plague when we move into their neighbourhoods. Is it any wonder, then, that their homes are suddenly and drastically reduced in value? They hastily abandon them, sacrificing them to the Bosses of the Buildings, the men who instigate all this for whatever profit they can get . . .

We watch strange moods fill our children, and our hearts swell with pain. The streets, with their noise and flaring lights, the taverns, the automobiles, and the pool rooms claim them, and no voice of ours can call them back. They spend their nights away from home; they forget our ways of life, our language, our God. Their swift speech and impatient eyes make us feel weak and foolish . . . We fall upon our knees and pray for them, but in vain. The city has beaten us, evaded us; but they, with young bodies filled with warm blood, feel bitter and frustrated at the sight of the alluring hopes and prizes denied them . . .

From 12 Million Black Voices; A Folk History of the Negro in the United States *by Richard Wright.*

Published by Viking Pess, New York, © 1941 Richard Wright; republished with accompanying photos by Thunder's Mouth Press, New York, 1988.

The American Dream and the American Negro (1965)

James Baldwin

It comes as a great shock to discover that the country which is your birthplace and to which you owe your life and identity has not, in its whole system of reality, evolved any place for you. The disaffection and the gap between people, only on the basis of their skins, begins there and accelerates throughout your whole lifetime. You realise that you are thirty and having a terrible time. You have been through a certain kind of mill and the most serious effect is again not the catalogue of disaster – the policeman, the taxi driver, the waiters, the landlady, the banks, the insurance companies, the millions of details twenty-four hours of every day which spell out to you that you are a worthless human being. It is not that. By that time you have begun to see it happening in your daughter, your son or your niece or your nephew. You are thirty by now and nothing you have done, and as far as you can tell nothing you can do, will save your son or daughter from having the same disaster and from coming to the same end.

> *From 'The American Dream and the American Negro',*
> The New York Times Magazine, *7 March 1965.*
> *Based on remarks by Baldwin in a debate held at*
> *the University of Cambridge, 18 February 1965.*

Nothing to Boast Of (1980)

Theodore Ward

As a young man, travelling across the United Sates, hoboing on a westbound freight train through the Rocky Mountains, I found myself at the Great Horseshoe Bend. Seated in the open doorway of the boxcar in which I was riding, I was enthralled by the overpowering beauty and strength of the towering hills, and the vast declivity to the valley beneath with its shrubbery of gold and red and brown bathed in the light of the sinking sun – the sides of the mountains themselves with their tall tress tinged with the amber of its dying rays and creating a sight of fabulous enchantment.

It seemed to me that such a scene had been the source of inspiration to the poet who had conceived of America as 'the beautiful'. My heart thrilled and I found myself singing of its 'purple mountain majesty above the fruited plain' as I had done as a child in school.

But suddenly I found my spirit sickened as I realised the truth: 'I'm a Negro and all this beauty and majesty does not belong to me.' With a fallen heart, I acknowledged that I had nothing to boast of. I was a descendant of the slaves who had built this country, yet I was still deprived of the patriotic joy felt by those who claimed the land as their own. In my bewilderment that late afternoon, it suddenly occurred to me that we as a people were engulfed by a pack of lies, surrounded, in fact, by one big white fog through which we could see no light anywhere. Disheartened, as the sun sank behind the mountains west of the Pass, I crawled back into a darkened corner of the boxcar and there I lay down, convinced that my life would be that of a 'floater', sans hope, sans purpose.

When *Big White Fog* was produced in the years before World War II, years of depression and disillusionment for black people, many were convinced that there was no hope for black liberation. Although much has changed, the Masons' struggle to discover the viable options through which to ameliorate their condition is as meaningful today as it was more than forty years ago.

Programme note for a reading of Big White Fog *in New York City in 1980.*

Key Dates

1915-20   The Great Migration. Up to 500,000 blacks leave the rural South and make their way to the cities of the North, pursuing the promise of a better life. By 1930 this figure is more than two million.

1916   Marcus Garvey arrives in the US from Jamaica.

1917   Garvey forms the first division of the Universal Negro Improvement Association (UNIA) in the US.

1918   End of World War One.

Garvey begins publication of *The Negro World* newspaper.

1919   Race riots erupt in twenty American cities, the largest and most violent in Chicago.

Garvey's Black Star Line is incorporated.

1920   The UNIA claims four million members.

25,000 fill Madison Square Garden, New York, to hear Garvey speak.

Prohibition established (not repealed till 1933).

1923   Having been pursued by the FBI, Garvey is convicted of mail fraud and sentenced to five years in prison.

1927   President Coolidge commutes his sentence and he is deported to Jamaica.

1929   The Great Crash on Wall Street (in October), leading to the economic and social disasters of the Great Depression (till 1934).

Big White Fog opened at the Great Northern Theatre, Chicago, on 7 April 1938, produced by the Negro Unit of the Chicago Federal Theatre Project.

Big White Fog received its European premiere at the Almeida Theatre, London, on 11 May 2007. The cast was as follows:

VICTOR MASON	Danny Sapani
ELLA	Jenny Jules
LESTER	Tunji Kasim
WANDA	Gugu Mbatha-Raw
CAROLINE	Ayesha Antoine
PHILLIP (older)	Nathan Stewart-Jarrett
DANIEL ROGERS	Tony Armatrading
JUANITA	Susan Salmon
MARTHA BROOKS	Novella Nelson
PERCY MASON	Clint Dyer
CLAUDINE	Lenora Crichlow
NATHAN PISZER	Aaron Brown
MARKS	Tony Turner
COUNT STRAWDER	Al Matthews
COUNT COTTON	Nathan Stewart-Jarrett
SISTER GABRELLA	Lenora Crichlow
BAILIFF	Glynn Sweet
LIEUTENANT	Tony Turner
PATROLMAN	Martin Barron
PHILLIP (younger)	Kedar Williams-Stirling / Victor Nyambe

Director   Michael Attenborough
Designer   Jonathan Fensom
Lighting Designer   Tim Mitchell
Sound Designer   John Leonard
Casting   Leo Davis

A Note on the Text

This text is an amalgamation of two original drafts of the play, not enormously different from each other. It also contains a few amendments to period slang words, whose meaning now is obscure.

I am hugely indebted to Laura Branca Ward, Theodore Ward's younger daughter, for her limitless support and help.

As this is perforce going to print prior to the first performance, it does not contain any small changes we may make during rehearsal.

Michael Attenborough
Artistic Director, Almeida Theatre

BIG WHITE FOG

Characters

VICTOR MASON (VIC), *a Garveyite leader*
ELLA, *his wife*
LESTER (LES), *their elder son*
WANDA, *their elder daughter*
CAROLINE, *their younger daughter*
PHILLIP, *their younger son*
DANIEL ROGERS, *their brother-in-law*
JUANITA, *Ella's sister, Daniel's wife*
MARTHA BROOKS, *mother of Ella and Juanita*
PERCY MASON, *brother of Victor*
CLAUDINE, *friend of Wanda*
NATHAN PISZER, *a student*
MARKS, *a used-furniture man*
COUNT STRAWDER, *Garveyite*
COUNT COTTON, *Garveyite*
SISTER GABRELLA, *a Black Cross nurse*
BAILIFF
LIEUTENANT
PATROLMAN

Bailiffs, Workers, Police

The play takes place in the home of Victor and Ella Mason on Dearborn Street, on Chicago's South Side.

Act One	*Scene One*	*An afternoon in August 1922*
	Scene Two	*One week later*
Act Two	*Scene One*	*One year later, August 1923*
	Scene Two	*The following January, 1924*
	Scene Three	*Early evening, one month later*
Act Three	*Scene One*	*Late afternoon, early August 1932*
	Scene Two	*Around 3 a.m., 31 August 1932*
	Scene Three	*Several hours later*

ACT ONE

Scene One

An afternoon in August, 1922.

Living room of the Masons, in Dearborn Street, Chicago. It is a large, congenial room, bearing the telltale signs of use, polished by care and indicating that people of means once lived here.

On the left, a large window with stained glass above and a window seat below. Beyond it, in the corner, is a hall-tree, and next to the latter, the front door, with a transom of stained glass of the same pattern. The light of a bright August sun.

Against the rear wall, a flight of stairs leads to the upper floor. Downstage right, a door leads into the kitchen and dining room.

There is a couch in the centre with an overstuffed chair to the left of it, and behind it an oblong table, against the stairway. A typewriter is on the table with a small chair at the left end of it.

A Victrola is against the right wall. Downstage left is another easy chair, and beyond it, near the window, a rocking chair, commanding a view of Fifty-first Street as it intersects Dearborn Street.

A postman's whistle sounds and ELLA *appears from the rear, going to the door where she retrieves a letter from the mailbox outside. As she re-enters, she stands fingering the letter and immersed in thought – a buxom mulatto, aged about thirty-eight and wearing a cool housedress.*

JUANITA *enters, unceremoniously, behind her. A good-looking mulatto, slender and smartly dressed, she has a decided verve of manner and vigour of speech.*

JUANITA. Hello, Ella.

ELLA (*startled*). Oh! Juanita – you like to scare me to death. What storm blew you to Dearborn Street?

JUANITA. Oh, I just thought I'd drop by to see how you all were. (*She turns to the mirror of the hall-tree in the corner behind her.*) What's that you got there, a notice from your landlord?

ELLA (*tossing letter on table beneath stairway*). No. It's for Les. Must be the answer about his scholarship.

JUANITA (*coming down*). No! (*Happily.*) You know, I'd almost forgotten about him entering for that scholarship!

ELLA (*going into rear*). Well, you wouldn't've if you lived around here.

JUANITA (*sitting on arm of couch and looking off right*). I suppose not. Well, I hope it's good news. (*Taking out cigarette.*)

ELLA *returns with a pan of green peas, which she takes to the couch and begins to shell.*

ELLA. They've kept him in suspense long enough. Did you bring Mama's pattern?

JUANITA. Lord, no! I knew there was something I was forgetting – (*Hiding cigarette quickly.*) Where is she?

ELLA (*laughing at her groundless fear*). Gone to the park. She took the children out for a breath of air.

JUANITA. If you had any sense you'd make Vic take a flat *near* the park.

ELLA. Juanita, you know we can't afford the rent.

JUANITA. You could if you made Vic go into partnership with Dan.

ELLA (*wearily*). It's no use starting that talk again. Vic's made up his mind about Africa, and there's nothing short of the voice of God likely to change him.

JUANITA. Ha! Ten years from today he'll still be in Chicago, carrying his hod.

ELLA. They've got over four million paid-up members!

JUANITA (*searching for ashtray*). It's nothing but bunk to catch more suckers like Vic.

ELLA. Vic's in the know, and he wouldn't lie to me. They've just made him a captain in the African Legionnaires.

JUANITA (*with an outburst of laughter*). Captain in the African Legionnaires – That's a good one!

ELLA. Stop your silly laughing, Vic's nobody's fool.

JUANITA. No? He's being taken for a ride just like the rest.

ELLA. That's all you know about it.

JUANITA. You don't see any of our really big people falling for Marcus Garvey's jive, do you?

ELLA. No. They're too jealous of his power!

JUANITA. You mean they've got too much sense to let a monkey-chasing crook like him come over here and jive them out of their cold cash!

ELLA. You make me sick. You can't see anything but money.

JUANITA. No. You're quite right, my dear. But I don't make any pretence about it.

ELLA. Is that an insinuation?

JUANITA. Ella, you know very well, if Vic was in the money, neither of you would give a damn about Africa.

ELLA. I haven't lived with Vic nineteen years for nothing. He cares about the race.

JUANITA. Yeah? Then he ought to be trying to do something for it here – like going in with Dan and opening that kitchenette. Our people are crying for some place to live, and they'll pay good money for the privilege.

ELLA. Vic's planning to buy shares in the Black Star Line, he can't spare –

JUANITA (*laughing*). The Black Star Line! Why, that's the biggest joke Marcus Garvey ever thought of – where're they going to get men to run it?

ELLA. From the West Indies –

JUANITA (*groaning*). Oh my God . . .

ELLA. Yeah, well, their steamship sails its maiden voyage from New York next week.

The door opens, and CAROLINE, *seeing her aunt, dashes in. She is a child of twelve, with long braids.*

CAROLINE. Aunt Juanita! I didn't know you was here!

JUANITA. *Was?*

PHILLIP *enters. He is a little black boy of ten.*

CAROLINE. Were –

JUANITA (*to* PHILLIP). Why haven't you been to see Aunt Juanita lately?

PHILLIP (*bouncing his ball*). We was over there last Wednesday, but you wasn't home –

JUANITA. Aunt Juanita is a pretty busy woman, honey – you should call me up and let me know when you're coming.

As PHILLIP's *ball gets away from him and he dashes behind couch to retrieve it,* JUANITA *sees her mother,* MARTHA BROOKS, *coming down, brusquely. A somewhat wizened mulatto, aged about sixty, she is much spryer than she pretends.*

Hello, Mama –

MARTHA. Move, Caroline! Lemme get off these feet!

JUANITA (*extinguishing her cigarette as* MARTHA *takes chair centre*). How're you feeling?

MARTHA. Them chillun jes 'bout wore me out, and what with the walk back from the park, I'm jes 'bout dead, I 'spect.

PHILLIP (*joining his mother on couch*). Grandma's been playing ball.

ELLA. Playing ball?

PHILLIP. Yes'm. We had a lot of fun, didn't we, Grandma?

JUANITA. Are you trying to kill yourself, Mama?

MARTHA. Now you all jes let me 'lone. And you get out of here, Phillip, with your big mouth.

ELLA. You'll be laid up for a week – why didn't you take the streetcar back, like I told you?

MARTHA (*to* JUANITA). Did you bring me mah pattern back?

JUANITA. I forgot it, Mama. But I'll get Les to bring it tomorrow.

MARTHA. Jes like I figgered. You so busy runnin' 'round smokin' and playin' cards, you can't remember nothing. I told you I needed that pattern so I could make Wanda's waist 'fore school opens!

JUANITA. Oh, calm yourself, Mama. You'll get it.

CAROLINE. Mama, may I have a slice of bread and butter?

PHILLIP (*springing up*). Me too, Mama?

ELLA. It's pretty near time for your dinner. But I reckon so –

As they run out rear:

And don't take but one apiece neither!

JUANITA (*playfully*). What's this, Mama, I hear about you planning to go to Africa?

MARTHA (*disgustedly*). Don't you mention no Africa to me, I'm sick o' hearin' it!

ELLA. For God's sake, Juanita – don't get her started.

JUANITA. Didn't you just tell me, Vic's made up his mind to go?

MARTHA. And I reckon you think 'cause I'm poor and can't help myself I got to go, hanh? Well, don't fool yourself. I ain't no Affikan; I'm a Dupree! I was born in this country and I'm going die in it, Vic or no Vic!

ELLA. Mama, nobody's trying to make you go anywhere!

MARTHA. No, and they better not be, I done let that black crank root me up once with his fool talk 'bout we goin' find freedom up here in the North. But he ain't goin' 'suade me again. I'se too old for another transplantin'.

ELLA (*exiting with the pan*). I guess you'd both rather be in Mississippi picking cotton – ?

JUANITA. Chicago's one thing, but Africa's another.

MARTHA. Yes, Lawd!

JUANITA. Vic'd forget that stuff too, Mama, if it wasn't for her encouraging him, like a fool!

MARTHA (*sighing*). She ain't got mah blood in her veins – No Dupree woulda thought 'bout marryin' sich a black crank in the first place.

ELLA (*re-enters angrily*). You and your Dupree blood! I've warned you, I'm sick of your flaunting Vic's colour in my face. If he's good enough to live on, you'll respect him.

JUANITA (*seeing* LES *through window*). Drop it, Ella – Here comes Les.

LES *enters, tossing his baseball glove on table. He is about twenty, in a white shirt and corduroy slacks.*

LES. Hello, Aunt Juanita!

JUANITA. Hi, Les!

ELLA. Your letter's here!

LES. My letter – where? (*He dives for the table.*)

MARTHA. What letter?

JUANITA. From his scholarship.

LES (*nervously, fingering letter*). This is it! This is it, all right.

JUANITA. You'll never know unless you read it.

MARTHA. No, he won't.

ELLA. Open it, Les.

LES *opens the letter and reads silently.*

JUANITA. What does it say?

ELLA. Yes, read it aloud, so we can all hear –

LES (*dancing a jig*). Hot dog! Hot ziggedy damn! (*Hugging his aunt.*) Oh boy, oh boy, oh boy!

ELLA. If you don't stop your foolishness and read that letter, Lester Mason, I'll pick up something and brain you!

LES. Wait, Mama, just listen to this. (*Reading, with suppressed emotion.*) 'Jason Scholarship Fund . . . Copeland Technical Institute, Kansas . . . '

ELLA. Oh, skip all that!

LES (*reading*). 'My dear Mr Mason . . . I have just returned from abroad to find your application for appointment as a Jason Scholar of Chemistry, and likewise the letter of Principal Horace Judson, confirming your record and recommending you for the award . . . '

JUANITA. Does that mean you get it?

LES. He says it's up to the Board – but listen. (*Reading*.) 'This, however, is of little consequence, when considering the high quality of your performance in chemistry, I am convinced favourable action will be taken; so that you can be with us this Fall . . . Yours truly, Rothmore C. Galen, Chairman, the Jason Scholarship Fund.'

JUANITA. Well, that's something!

ELLA. I'm so glad, Les. (*Her eyes brim and she wipes away a tear of joy*.)

MARTHA. Don't seem to say a thing to me.

JUANITA. It means he's certain to go to college, Mama.

MARTHA. Seems like a mighty poor way of saying it.

JUANITA. And you say it's for four years, Les?

LES. If my marks are good.

ELLA. Your father will be tickled to death.

JUANITA. Who wouldn't be? It should make him see this country in a better light.

LES. Oh, Papa's all right. I won't be the first Negro to receive a scholarship –

He catches sight of WANDA, *his very pretty sister, and joins her.*

What d'you think, Wanda? I just got an answer from my application!

WANDA. About your scholarship?

LES. Yeah. Looks like I'm Kansas-bound.

As WANDA *goes to the table to examine mail, her attitude belies the happiness of the others, as well as the fact she's only seventeen.*

ELLA. Well, can't you say anything?

WANDA (*turning, embarrassed*). I was just thinking, Mama – (*Quickly.*) but I'm glad you got it, Les. I knew you would. When do you leave?

LES (*relieved, bringing her to chair*). I don't know yet. Everything's not really settled. Here – (*Gives her letter.*) Read it for yourself.

JUANITA (*as* WANDA *reads*). Four years! (*Impishly.*) Your father'll have to leave you here, won't he?

LES (*puzzled*). What d'you mean, Aunt?

JUANITA. He's going to Africa, isn't he?

ELLA. Oh, stop teasing him, Juanita – Les, isn't it time for you to be getting out on your route?

LES. Lord, I had completely forgotten my papers! (*Going.*) See you all later. (*Suddenly turning back to* WANDA.) Give me that – (*To all.*) And don't you all say anything to Papa, will you? I want to surprise him.

He exits running.

ELLA. All right. We won't.

MARTHA. He sure is tickled pink.

JUANITA. With a fine break like that, he'll be a big man some day.

MARTHA (*sourly*). Yeah. If he don't turn out like his pa.

ELLA (*to* WANDA). Perhaps you'll win one this year.

JUANITA. There's no reason why she shouldn't with the brain she's got.

WANDA (*drily*). Thanks, Aunt. But I'm not interested in any scholarship.

ELLA. What do you mean?

WANDA (*rising and going*). Oh, nothing.

ELLA (*arresting her*). Don't tell me. You did mean something?

JUANITA. Yes, she did. (*To* WANDA.) Surely you aren't jealous of your own brother?

WANDA (*sarcastically*). Jealous! Don't kid me, Aunt Juanita. Les is perfectly welcome to the scholarship.

ELLA. You don't act like it.

JUANITA. She certainly doesn't. I've been watching her ever since she came in.

WANDA. What am I supposed to do, shed tears over it?

JUANITA. You ought to be proud to see him get such a break.

WANDA. It's a fine break all right – marvellous – splendid! (*Bitterly*.) When he gets out of school, maybe they'll give him a job on the dining car figuring out how many calories there are in the average bowl of soup!

ELLA. Wanda!

JUANITA. Well, did you ever!

WANDA. You needn't pretend to be so astonished, either of you –

JUANITA (*sharply*). Why, you're crazy. The field of chemistry is wide open to our people. Look at Dr Carver!

WANDA. Yeah, Dr Carver! One out of a million! But what about Papa? Tuskegee graduate, carrying a hod! And Uncle Dan, Butler's Black Pride, working on a Pullman car!

ELLA (*feebly*). Your father was educated to be a farmer.

WANDA. That's it. He's a farmer, but where's his farm?

JUANITA (*hesitantly*). But . . . but your Uncle Dan's working for a purpose.

WANDA. They're both just kidding themselves. (*Turning to* ELLA.) You might as well know it right now, Mama, I'm not going back to school!

ELLA. Is that so? Since when did you get big enough to tell me to my face what you're not going to do?

MARTHA. She needs slapping down!

WANDA. I'm no longer a child, Grandma!

MARTHA (*outraged*). Oh, if you was only mine, I'd take you down a buttonhole lower.

WANDA. But I happen not to be yours, Grandma!

MARTHA. Ella, are you goin' stand there and let her sassy me like this?

ELLA (*jerking* WANDA *round*). Stop your impudence and answer me!

WANDA. Well, you had to know sooner or later. I'm sick of school, and there's no use in your trying to send me back.

ELLA. Is that so?

JUANITA. Wanda, if you quit school you'll never amount to anything – you won't even be able to make a decent marriage.

WANDA. I'm not interested in marriage. I'm going to work.

JUANITA. And what kind of job do you suppose you're going to find?

WANDA. I've already got one.

ELLA. Doing what?

WANDA. Claudine's going to get me on with her . . . as soon as the other girl goes back to school.

ELLA (*incredulously*). In the drugstore?

WANDA. Yes. The boss has already told me I'll do. I'm the type.

JUANITA. Jerkin' soda! My own niece meeting every tramp who takes a notion to buy a bottle of pop.

MARTHA. I warned you, Ella, I told you 'bout lettin' her run round with that fast Claudine!

JUANITA. Can't you see if you go on, you could at least teach school?

WANDA. Teach school! Aunt, you make me laugh!

ELLA. What's wrong with that?

WANDA. Mama, you know yourself how much our people are kicking against coloured teachers.

JUANITA. But a drugstore? Why, why . . . it's positively ridiculous!

WANDA. I don't care. I've as much right to nice things as anyone else. If I go to work I can get them.

ELLA. So you think you've been neglected, hunh? I'd like to know who you think around here looks any better than you do?

MARTHA. Nobody. There ain't a girl on this street looks any better.

WANDA. Yeah. I'm all right on Dearborn Street. But alongside the girls over East I look like mud.

JUANITA. But I always try to help you, don't I?

WANDA. Yes. And I thank you, Aunt Juanita. But I'm tired of wearing cast-off things.

JUANITA. Well!

WANDA. I want to be independent. In two months I'll be a full-grown woman, and I'm going to live!

MARTHA. What you mean, you 'goin' live'?

WANDA (*going*). Oh, you wouldn't understand, Grandma.

MARTHA. No, I'm too old, you little hussy. I ain't got sense enough. But it might surprise you to know, you pigheaded little wench, I said them same words to mah mammy 'fore yours was born!

WANDA. Then I don't see why you asked.

ELLA (*quietly*). Maybe your mother's just a back number, too, darling. But she'd like to know.

WANDA (*animatedly*). Get some joy out of life, Mama! Have clothes and be able to go places and do things, like Uncle Percy!

MARTHA (*disgustedly*). The drunken bum! Your Uncle Percy's a disgrace to the family. Do you think just because he wears good clothes and sleeps in the cabarets, he's livin'?

WANDA. At least he's not kidding himself like the rest of the family. He knows there's nothing for us in this country. The white folks proved it, too, when they ripped his uniform off his back when he came home from France!

JUANITA. You can't hold all the white people guilty for the act of a few hoodlums! Nor is it any excuse for his throwing himself away!

WANDA. Uncle Percy's living so when he gets old he won't have anything to regret.

ELLA. Nothing to regret, hunh?

WANDA. There's nothing in this country for a Negro girl to look forward to, and you know it as well as I. You and Papa might as well get used to the idea. Because whether you like it or not, I'm going to live my own life – even if I have to leave here! (*She runs out.*)

She goes as VICTOR MASON *enters from the front door. He is a tall, very black man, dressed in an old suit, his hands stained with mortar – but his dignified bearing and keen eyes show him to be a man of considerable intelligence and character. He turns to* ELLA.

VIC. What's the matter with her?

ELLA. Nothing, Vic.

VIC. Wanda's not in trouble, is she?

MARTHA. No. But if you don't watch out she's goin' be!

VIC. Ella, what is this?

ELLA. Wanda's going to quit school.

VIC. Is that so?

ELLA. Says she's going to work so she can *live*!

VIC (*going to hall-tree to hang hat*). Well, I don't see anything to get excited about. Let her quit.

ELLA (*shocked*). Let her quit? You mean that?

VIC. Sure. What difference does it make? They're only filling her head with a stack of white folks' lies anyway.

JUANITA. White folks' lies!

VIC. There isn't a word of truth about a black man in all her books put together!

MARTHA. If that don't prove you's cranky-headed, I dunno what will.

ELLA (*to* VIC). Have you lost your reason?

VIC. I see exactly what I'm talking about.

ELLA. Oh, you do?

She sees CAROLINE *and* PHILLIP *entering.*

Go get ready for your dinner.

As the children ascend stairs, she continues bitterly:

And I suppose I haven't got anything to say about it, huh?

VIC. It isn't that, Ella. You don't quite understand. I'm . . .

ELLA. No. (*Bitterly.*) Well, you just go right ahead. Let her quit. She's yours. Let her ruin herself. Let her slide down to hell!

JUANITA. Now you're talking, Ella. Any father in his right mind –

VIC (*sharply*). Now, wait a minute, both of you. Give me a moment to explain – and I promise you –

ELLA (*furiously*). I don't want to hear any explanations or promises either – I've had enough of them. You brought me out of the South with one – you and your fine talk about freedom and giving the children a chance to be somebody!

VIC (*injuredly*). I'm sorry you feel that way about it, Ella. I know I haven't done all I promised. But you know as well as I do, I'm not to blame –

ELLA. I'll get a lot of comfort out of that!

VIC. I'm still trying, ain't I? What do you think I'm carrying a hod by day and wrestling in the movement all night for? Wanda's just reached the point where she sees what we're up against in this country. (*Turning to the stairs.*) Be patient a little longer. (*Halting as he starts up.*) We'll soon be out of this rut and on our way to Africa. It won't be long now. You're going to see the black man come out of the darkness of failure into the light of achievement with the cloak of human greatness about his shoulders . . . Yes, Lord! And our enemies shall tremble when he stretches forth his mighty hand to gather in his share of the God-given stars of glory!

Leaving them, he disappears above.

ELLA (*helplessly*). What can you do with a man like that?

Curtain.

Scene Two

Saturday afternoon, a week later.

LES *is seated in the window, reading a book. After a moment* PERCY *descends, wearing a gaudy silk dressing gown. A handsome brown man, he stretches like a panther as he reaches the floor, and comes out of it with a grunt.*

PERCY. Phumph! Reading again, hunh?

LES. Yep.

PERCY. That's all you ever do . . . (*Going out rear*.) You're getting to be a regular sissy. (*Returning shortly with a glass of water*.) Where's everybody?

LES. Out, I guess – except Wanda. Mama and Grandma went shopping. Caroline and Phillip are out there playing.

PERCY (*takes a pint of gin from pocket of robe and places it on end table of couch*). I gotta have some ginger ale. (*Crosses to window to call*.) Phillip! . . . Come here a minute, will you? (*Takes coin from pocket*.)

PHILLIP *enters*.

PERCY (*giving him a coin*). Here. Run get me a bottle of ginger ale. And hurry now –

PHILLIP *runs out*.

Lawd, my head feels like a keg of nails. (*He pours a drink, then goes to table to search through papers*.) Umph. No mail! (*He goes back to couch to drink his liquor and chase it with water*.) What kind of a book did you say that was?

LES. I didn't.

PERCY (*sharply*). No! Well, what is it, then – love story?

LES. No. It's a book Papa gave me.

PERCY. Yeah – what's the name of it?

LES. *Looking Backward* by Edward Bellamy.

PERCY. Never heard of it.

LES. No. It isn't likely.

PERCY. Now just what did you mean by that?

LES. Nothing, Uncle Percy – only it's not exactly a novel.

PERCY (*rising and going to window*). Oh, what is it, then?

LES. It's a book on socialism.

PERCY. What?

LES (*smiling*). Surprised?

PERCY. Socialism! Your daddy'll make a nut out of you yet. (*Going back to couch.*) Have you heard any more from the school?

LES. Not yet. But I ought to get a letter any day now.

PERCY. Do you think you'll get it?

LES. I don't see any reason why I shouldn't. I got an 'A' out of the course.

PERCY (*pouring another drink*). I don't know what good it'll do you, from what I've seen of the rest of the educated bigshots in this family. But I guess you'll need clothes. You can have that pin-striped grey suit of mine and the brown you say you like so well.

LES. Aw, you're kidding me, Uncle Percy!

PERCY. You got to tog down if you want to go places –

LES. Hot pajamas!

PERCY. If I have any luck at the hotel this week, I'll set you up to a new one. With the three you ought to be sharp as a tack when you hit that campus.

LES. Lord, Lord, are you telling me!

> PHILLIP *enters with ginger ale.*

PERCY. You sure took your time.

PHILLIP. They was busy. (*He offers change.*)

PERCY (*waving change away*). That's all right.

PHILLIP (*gleefully, running out*). Thank you, Uncle Percy!

> CLAUDINE *enters, a pretty girl of eighteen wearing a summer frock.*

CLAUDINE (*encountering* PHILLIP). Hey! Look out!

> *Exit* PHILLIP.

LES. Oh, hello, Claudine!

CLAUDINE. Hi! Wanda home?

LES. Yes, sure – I'll call her.

> *He runs upstairs, as* CLAUDINE *saunters in. Suddenly determined to try her wiles on the older man, she removes her gum.*

CLAUDINE. What're you doing, Uncle Percy – having a ball all by yourself?

PERCY. Just trying to give my aching head a break. Have a . . . some ginger ale?

CLAUDINE (*laughing slyly*). Don't play me cheap, big boy. I've been around!

PERCY (*amused*). Oh, you have!

CLAUDINE. I saw you in the Dreamland last week – and were you *high*!

PERCY (*surprised*). You, in the Dreamland – ?

CLAUDINE. Sure – only –

PERCY. Only what?

CLAUDINE. Oh, the kids I run with only go for the notoriety. Three highballs and they pass out.

PERCY (*slyly probing*). Sure 'nough! Can't Wanda take it either?

CLAUDINE. Wanda's too scared to go anywhere – but why don't you take me sometime?

PERCY. Me, take you cabareting?

CLAUDINE. What's the matter – (*Laughing*.) Ain't I hot enough for you? (*She whirls as a model before him*.)

PERCY. Oh, sure.

CLAUDINE. You don't act like it.

PERCY. You're too young for me, kid. I'm a tough papa.

CLAUDINE (*resting her knee on chair*). I'm nineteen, almost – and don't think I can't take care of myself!

PERCY. You're a keen little chick all right. But you'd better give Les a break.

CLAUDINE. I can't be bothered with the cradle –

She laughs as she sees WANDA *descending*.

Hi, kiddo! Are you ready?

VIC *enters in his good suit*.

WANDA. Yes, come on. (*Greeting her father*.) Hello, Papa.

VIC. Well, you're certainly looking cool, Claudine. How's your folks?

CLAUDINE. Everybody's well, thank you.

WANDA. Papa, Claudine and I are going to Forty-Seventh Street.

VIC. Well, be sure you're back in time for dinner.

WANDA (*going*). OK, Papa.

CLAUDINE (*saucily*). Don't forget what I told you, Uncle Percy.

She exits with WANDA.

WANDA (*as they disappear*). What's this between you and . . . ?

VIC (*indicating gin*). At it again?

PERCY. Take it easy, Captain –

Outside, DAN, *a brown man aged about thirty-seven, immaculately groomed, is heard exchanging greeting with the girls.*

DAN (*appearing in front door*). Well, how's everybody?

VIC. Just fine, Dan. And how're you?

DAN (*coming downstage*). Never felt better nor had less in my life. (*Seeing* LES *descending.*) I hear you're fixing to leave us, Les.

LES. Not for sure, Uncle Dan. I haven't received the final word yet.

DAN. You'll get it. Just get yourself in the right frame of mind to make the best of your chance.

PERCY. You needn't worry about him – (*Offering drink.*) Have a little snort?

DAN (*taking chair*). No, thanks.

PERCY. You're getting to be as big a heel as Vic. How's the railroad?

DAN. Things are picking up right along. I had eight carriages all the way from Los Angeles. How's tricks on the bellstand?

PERCY. They ain't walking no more.

DAN. No? – And you, Vic?

VIC. My hod ain't getting no lighter. But the movement's swinging along.

DAN. I hear you're planning a World Conference!

VIC. How did you know?

DAN. I picked up one of your big shots in Denver, on his way to the Coast – (*Laughing.*) Called himself the Duke of the Niger!

VIC (*unamused*). Yeah?

DAN. Yeah. Talk about a spade. He sure was one for you. Kept the car in an uproar all the way to Los Angeles.

PERCY. Clowning for the whites, hunh?

DAN (*emphatically*). And how!

PERCY (*acrimoniously*). I could drown that kind in a tub of carbolic!

DAN. Me too. Made me so sick I wanted to throw him out the window.

VIC (*incredulously*). And you say he was a Garveyite?

DAN. That's what he claimed.

LES. What did he say?

DAN. What didn't he say! 'Jerusalem for the Jew!' he kept preaching, with the white folks egging him on; 'Ireland for the Irish, and Africa for the Africans!' – It was disgusting. I doubt if it ever occurred to him he was playing right into the white man's hands.

VIC. How's that?

DAN. By telling them just what they want to hear – advocating segregation!

VIC. You don't understand the new spirit, Dan. We're out to wrest our heritage from the enemy.

DAN. What '*our*'? My heritage is right here in America!

VIC (*quietly*). What? A lynch rope?

DAN. Like hell. If those chumps down South haven't got sense enough to get out from under, they ought to be strung up.

VIC. You talk like an imbecile, Dan. Have you forgotten East St Louis, Tulsa, Washington? And what they did to Percy there when he came back from France?

DAN. I haven't forgotten anything. But all this agitation doesn't mean a thing. You can't do anything for people who don't care anything about themselves. You only stir up strife. Let them alone, I say, and try to get something out of them for yourself. There's chance enough for anybody in this country if he's got get-up enough to take it.

PERCY. Yeah. A chance to be doormats for the white folks' feet!

DAN. Doormats my eye. Outwit the white man. Get something in your pocket and stop expecting the millennium!

VIC. You know what, Dan? It just strikes me what's wrong with educated Negroes like you.

DAN. Oh, yeah! Give me the benefit of your great wisdom.

VIC. Your education is like a pair of kneepads. It enables you to crawl through the slime of white prejudice without the least sense of pain or dishonour!

DAN (*stung*). If I didn't know you so well, I'd . . . You can't see, the only difference between your feelings and mine is simply a matter of control.

VIC. Of course, with the help of your education.

DAN. You bet. I've got too much sense to let prejudice blind me to the thing that counts in this world. Get your share of the loot, and all else will be added unto you!

VIC. We're all the same to the white man, rich or poor. What I want is freedom here and now!

DAN. So do I. But I say, first get the cash.

PERCY. By crawling on your belly?

DAN. A man can do business with his own people, can't he? Take this proposition of mine now, Vic. Everywhere you turn, our people are looking for a place to live – it's the chance of a lifetime –

VIC. You're still just thinking about yourself.

DAN (*earnestly*). Even so, man. You're not going to Africa tomorrow, are you? And you can't deny you'll need money when you do go. Come in with me. Opening this kitchenette will make us both public benefactors.

VIC. You mean public beneficiaries!

PERCY. I don't know, Captain. As long as we've got to be bled by somebody, I'd rather it be a black man.

DAN. Now you're talking sense, Percy.

VIC (*hotly*). Bunk. Mixed up with the white man as we are, Africa is the only solution.

DAN. But what about temporarily, just to help me get started – ?

VIC. I'm backing the Garvey Movement, Dan. Right this minute I'm expecting the committee to bring me some stock – shares in the Black Star Line that we're trying to open up between here and Africa.

DAN. Shucks, Vic. In six months we'll be sitting so pretty, you'll be able to purchase all the stock you want and then some.

VIC. Sure – so you say!

DAN. I've figured it all out, I tell you. We can lease a six-flat building for $400 a month. We'll cut it up into forty apartments that'll rent for twenty bucks apiece. That's an income of $800 a month – or $200 each after the lease is paid. Where're you going to beat that?

PERCY. That's a lot of dough.

MARTHA *enters from the front door and heads for her favourite rocker.*

MARTHA. Make room you all and lemme git off these feet!

ELLA (*entering behind her, her arms full of parcels*). Here, Les, make yourself useful.

LES (*joining her and taking parcels*). Did you bring the paper?

ELLA (*tossing Negro newspaper,* The Chicago Defender, *on table*). Yes – there it is.

Exit LES into rear with parcels.

DAN. Looks like you're planning to open a grocery store.

ELLA (*following LES out back*). We need one to feed this family.

She exits.

DAN. You're sure looking well, Mama.

MARTHA (*pleased at being noticed*). I'm doing pretty fair, thank the Lawd – though I'm tired out right now.

DAN. Juanita said hello. (*Turning back to* VIC.) As I was saying – if we put in $1,500 apiece, we can furnish the building from top –

VIC. But $1,500 –

DAN. We've got to avoid credit, and start off with a clean slate.

VIC. That's just about every single cent I own – !

LES re-enters to pick up the newspaper, crosses to window seat and begins reading.

DAN. What difference does it make? You'll have your principal back in eight months!

VIC (*going*). I'll have to think about it. I've got to get into my uniform before the committee comes. (*He goes up the stairs.*)

DAN. It's the chance of your lifetime. Don't forget that.

VIC. So you say! (*Exits above.*)

PERCY (*to DAN, chuckling*). He's sure salty, ain't he?

DAN. As a pickled herring.

LES (*springing up, excitedly*). For crying out loud! (*Coming forward.*) Listen to this . . . Where's Papa?

DAN. Upstairs. What is it?

LES (*reading*). 'Black Star Liner Halted at Pier!'

PERCY. Halted? What for?

DAN. No! (*Joining LES.*) Lemme see!

LES (*as another takes paper*). Lord, Lord – I wonder what Papa's going to say!

MARTHA. What is it, Les?

LES. They've stopped the *Republic* from sailing.

MARTHA. To Affiki – How come?

PERCY. Read it out, Dan.

DAN (*laughing*). This is a scream –

He strides to foot of stairs to shout.

Vic! Vic! Come on down here! Wait till he gets an earful of this. If he ain't a lucky man, the Sante Fe's a bus line!

ELLA (*re-entering*). What's going on here?

DAN. They've stopped that piece of junk of Marcus Garvey's from sailing.

ELLA. My God! Who stopped it?

DAN. The government, that's who.

VIC (*appearing above*). What's the trouble?

DAN (*going up to foot of stairs*). Come down here and take a look at this.

VIC *descends, buttoning the jacket of his Garvey uniform.*

I told you a man'd be a fool to trust that monkey-chaser – (*Handing* VIC *the paper.*) Read this –

STRAWDER, *a heavy-set black man of forty, appears in the doorway, with another,* COTTON, *behind him. Both are dressed in the regalia of the Garveyites – a black uniform trimmed with red, and white, plumed helmets.*

STRAWDER. Good evening, folks!

ELLA (*turning*). Oh, good evening, Mr Strawder – come in, won't you?

VIC (*oblivious of all*). It's a lie! A dirty rotten lie!

ELLA. Vic!

VIC. Excuse me, gentlemen. I didn't see you come in.

STRAWDER. Is anything wrong, Captain Mason?

VIC. Here, Les, read this for me, son.

LES. 'Black Star Liner halted at Pier – '

COTTON. What's that?

LES (*reading*). 'New York – As the Black Star Line steamship *Republic* prepared to sail on its maiden voyage today, passengers aboard and spectators on the crowded Hudson River pier were thrown into panic, culminating in near riot, when Maritime Inspector Davis O'Rouke declared the boat unseaworthy and issued orders forbidding the Captain from clearing port – '

STRAWDER. Great God A'mighty!

VIC. Sit down, Count Strawder. Read on, Les.

LES (*reading*). 'Inspection came as a result of rumours which recently began circulating in Harlem that leaders of the co-operative enterprise had been fleeced, when they purchased the giant craft at a cost of approximately a million dollars, despite the fact that the antiquated ship had not been in commission since the World War – '

DAN (*laughing derisively*). Wouldn't that squeeze you!

LES (*continuing*). 'It was reported that Marcus Garvey, Provisional President of the proposed Black Republic of Africa, and leader of the movement, had taken flight to Canada.'

STRAWDER (*with an air of despair*). No!

VIC. It's a lie – a dirty trick!

DAN. A trick – ?

MARTHA (*derisively*). It's a trick all right. That Marcus Garvey's done tricked the folks out o' their money – talkin' bout a *black* land for the *black* man!

VIC. Hush, Mama! You don't understand.

MARTHA. Don't tell me I don't understand! I told you he wasn't no good, and when I tell a pusson somethin' they can take it for granted. If I tell you a chicken dip snuff, jes look under her wing and you'll find the box!

DAN *explodes with irrepressible laughter*.

VIC (*angrily*). What do you think this is, a circus? This is no laughing matter. This is a white frame-up. They think if they discredit our leader, they'll bust up the movement!

DAN (*staggered*). Are you crazy, Vic? That inspector was a government man!

VIC. That's just what I mean.

COTTON. And you think Uncle Sam had a hand in it?

DAN. Tommy rot! If Washington cared anything about that monkey-chaser, they'd kick him back to the islands so fast they'd make his head spin.

VIC. Listen, the big men run this country, don't they? Haven't they got everything to gain by destroying the confidence of our members?

The postman's whistle sounds..

LES (*heading for door*). The mailman! . . .

He meets WANDA *entering with letter.*

Who's it for?

WANDA *hands him the letter.*

(*Going downstage left.*) This is it! Papa!

PERCY. From the scholarship?

WANDA. Ugh-hunh.

VIC (*explaining to others*). My boy won a scholarship to
college, and that's the letter about it.

ELLA (*seeing pain on boy's face*). What's the matter . . . ?
Is . . . ?

LES (*biting his lip*). Well, I guess . . . it's all off!

VIC. What?

ELLA. Oh, God!

WANDA (*her eyes swimming*). You don't mean . . .

She joins him to take letter.

LES (*crossing to chair*). I happen to be a little too black, I guess.

ELLA (*unbelievingly*). There *must* be some mistake –

DAN (*taking letter from* WANDA). Let me see!

PERCY *joins* DAN *as he takes a step toward the couch, to
read aloud.*

(*Reading.*)'My dear Mr Mason, I have been instructed to
inform you that on the basis of information received from
one in your community, stating that you are a Negro – '

PERCY (*reading over his shoulder*). ' – the board has no other
alternative than to deny your application, since under the
provisions of the late Mr Jason's will, the executors are
expressly constrained from making any monies available to
members of your race – ' The dirty bastards!

WANDA (*going to* LES). I'm so sorry, Les!

ELLA. It isn't fair! God, you know it isn't fair!

PERCY (*going upstage left, angrily*). The only fair thing about a white man is the colour of his skin!

VIC (*nodding his head slowly*). Nobody else could be guilty of such a cheap, petty – (*Hoarsely, to* LES.) But it's all right, boy!

DAN (*darkly*). I wish I could put my hands on the one who told them he was coloured!

MARTHA. Somebody round here.

STRAWDER. Did that out of jealousy.

COTTON. One of our own people!

VIC. They would've found out anyway, soon's he arrived – (*Resolutely.*) But this settles it! (*To* STRAWDER.) Got your subscription list handy, Count?

ELLA. What're you fixing to do?

VIC (*searching for his breast pocket, forgetful that he's wearing uniform*). Answer my son's letter – are you with me?

ELLA. You know I am. But what're you – ?

VIC. Wanda, run upstairs and get me my cheque book.

DAN (*as she runs up*). But Vic . . . !

VIC. Get your list out, Count!

DAN. Ella!

She is silent, and he turns back to VIC, *sensing the futility of his action.*

Oh, I know how you feel, Vic, but you can't afford to let this thing drive you to anything so rash.

STRAWDER (*at end of table, with pen and papers*). How many shares you going to take, Captain?

VIC (*firmly*). Fifteen hundred!

DAN. But Vic. It's worthless, man!

VIC (*quietly*). To you, perhaps.

DAN. This is madness! . . . Wait, Vic. Wait until you feel better. Let it go until tomorrow at least!

VIC. You and your 'tomorrow'. Will you never stop talking about tomorrow? Can't nothing make you see there's none for us in this Godforsaken country?

WANDA *returns to hand him his cheque book.*

Thanks.

He makes out a cheque.

DAN (*to* ELLA). Are you going to be a fool, too? Can't you see what he's doing? Speak to him!

PERCY (*exploding, bitterly*). Speak to him! Speak to him! What do you want her to say? Tell him to drop everything and stay here and let these dirty, damn hypocrites tear the hearts out of the rest of his children?

He exits above.

ELLA (*in tears*). I'd rather choke first!

DAN (*surrendering*). All right. All right. If you're going to let bitterness get the best of you, it's your funeral – But don't say I didn't warn you. (*Going.*) With that damn steamship nothing but junk, that stock isn't worth the paper it's printed on!

He exits to street.

VIC (*handing cheque to* STRAWDER). Here you are, Count.

STRAWDER (*rising*). I made out three certificates for $500 each.

MARTHA (*in despair*). Lawd! Lawd! Lawd!

VIC (*taking shares*). Thanks.

STRAWDER (*extending his hand*). Don't thank me, Captain Mason. I don't deserve it. I'm going to write to our leader and tell him how you're sticking by him in this hour of need.

VIC. It's a poor man that needs to be thanked for following the star of his people's destiny, Count.

STRAWDER (*going, he dons his helmet*). Well – Gooday!

He walks with dignity towards the door. ELLA *sinks onto the couch in silent tears.*

VIC. Don't cry, Ella!

For a moment his hand rests upon her shoulder.

LES (*bewildered, staring upon the world with an inward eye*). Seems like the world ain't nothing but a big white fog, and we can't see no light nowhere!

ELLA *sobs.*

VIC (*with a sense of compassion for his wounded son*). Look to the East, son, and keep on looking! Africa, the sun of our hope, is rising!

The curtain falls slowly.

ACT TWO

Scene One

August, a year later.

Everything is as we saw it last, except that now WANDA *is seated at the oblong table, typing, as her father dictates from a batch of notes.*

MARTHA *occupies the rocker, watching the doings on the street through the window;* ELLA *is sewing, mending the jacket of* VIC*'s uniform.*

There is the steady rhythm of WANDA*'s typing for a moment following the rise of the curtain, then she looks up at her father inquiringly.*

VIC (*dictating, in response to her glance*). 'And thus we shall eventually be able to build an agrarian co-operative economy – '

WANDA. How do you spell agrarian?

VIC. A-g-r-a-r-i-a-n.

She nods.

' – agrarian co-operative economy of lasting benefit to the Republic.' Paragraph.

ELLA (*preoccupied*). How long do you think the strike will last, Vic?

VIC (*casually*). A month or so, maybe . . . (*Dictating.*) 'Unfortunately – '

ELLA (*anxiously*). That long – ?

VIC. Never mind, Ella. Let the strike drop.

ELLA. I was just thinking how Les is going to feel if you leave him behind?

WANDA. That's right, Papa. He's going to be awfully disappointed, the way he's been boasting for weeks of going with you to Harlem.

VIC. I can't help that. We can't afford it. This is a general
    walkout – painters, bricklayers, plasterers and all – I
    wouldn't think of making the trip if I hadn't promised this
    paper – (*To* WANDA.) Where were we?

WANDA. 'Unfortunately – '

MARTHA (*looking out window*). Here's Les now.

VIC (*going on*). 'Unfortunately, the hostile nature of the
    Negro's environment in the agricultural South does not
    permit of experimentation there.' Period. 'Otherwise – '

LES (*entering upstage left, excitedly*). You know what, Papa?
    Uncle Dan is just as dirty as he can be. He just put one of
    his tenants out this afternoon and she hasn't any place to
    stay!

VIC. Is that so?

LES. He set her right out on the sidewalk 'cos her rent was
    three weeks overdue, and Mrs Davis was a nice woman too.

ELLA. Three weeks? That all?

LES. You don't know Uncle Dan, Mama. He's hard as they
    make 'em. He usually puts a plug in their doorlock in
    twenty-four hours.

WANDA. So he reckoned himself giving her a break, huh?

LES. Yeah. I guess so. Maybe because she has a baby and her
    husband ran off with another woman.

VIC. Dan has no more conscience than a bedbug.

LES. For two cents I wouldn't go back to work for him – you
    ought to have seen her sitting on the sidewalk crying.

ELLA. There ought to be a law – What's the poor soul going
    to do . . . Was she young?

LES. About twenty-five, I guess.

MARTHA. I reckon she'll make it, then.

VIC. And he wanted me to be his partner!

WANDA. Was Aunt Juanita there?

LES. No. But it wouldn't've made any difference; the way she
    lays on everybody about their rent –

MARTHA (*strangely excited*). Here they come, now, driving a brand new car!

WANDA (*springing up from chair and crossing to join her*). New car?

ELLA *follows suit.*

LES. I forgot to tell you.

WANDA. Come see, Papa.

ELLA. My, but it's beautiful! What kind of a car is it, Les?

LES. A Cadillac!

MARTHA. Lawd, a Cadillac!

VIC (*crossing to look*). Phumph! (*Turning back, displeased.*) No mystery how he got it.

JUANITA (*entering*). Well, are the travellers ready?

ELLA (*going back to seat*). Not quite. Come on in, you all.

DAN (*entering*). See my new boat, Vic?

VIC. Yeah. And from the looks of it, you don't have to tell me your kitchenettes are making money.

DAN. Just thought I'd make Juanita a little present. But it's costing me plenty. Thirty-eight hundred bucks is a lot of money, take it from Daniel.

MARTHA. Thirty-eight hund'd dollars – Lawdy!

JUANITA (*laughing*). How do you like it, Mama?

MARTHA. Lawd, chile, it's out of this world.

WANDA. You must be tickled to death, Aunt.

JUANITA (*going to window seat*). Oh, I'm not shedding any tears, dear!

DAN (*sitting*). I reckon not. Say, Vic, aren't you making a mistake taking Les to New York? I really need him, and you know yourself he'll need every cent he can earn if he's going to enter the U this fall?

VIC (*with a tinge of bitterness*). Well, you can ease your mind on that score –

As LES *reacts.*

I'm sorry, Les. I was just going to tell you . . . The strike –

DAN. A strike!

VIC. The contractors are defiant! And . . . er . . . you see, Les –
Well, I don't know just how long I may be out of work, so –

LES (*crestfallen*). You can't spare the money!

VIC. I wouldn't go myself if I didn't have a role at the
conference.

LES. If you haven't got the money, you just haven't, that's all.

DAN. Attaboy, Les, in a few years you'll be able to take a trip
around the world – once you get your education.

ELLA (*covering the situation*). Hadn't you better finish your
paper, Vic?

VIC. Yes, yes. Of course. (*To* JUANITA *and* DAN.) Excuse
me, will you – I've only got a paragraph or two more.

DAN. Les was telling me about it. What's the subject?

VIC. 'The Outlook for Co-operative Farming in Africa.'

DAN. Sounds interesting.

VIC. Read the last sentence back to me, Wanda.

WANDA (*at machine*). 'Unfortunately, the hostile nature of the
Negro's environment in the agricultural South does not
permit of experimentation there. Otherwise – '

VIC. Oh, yeah. (*Dictating.*) 'Otherwise it would be distinctly
advantageous to try out the plan here,' comma, 'as it might
easily prove the solution of the race problem in this
country.' Period. 'For should the Negro successfully wrest
his economic independence from his white oppressors,'
comma, 'their attitude of superiority would inevitably
disappear, since it would then no longer possess any basis
in reality. But this is, of course, merely to indulge in
fortuitous wishing; so I am emboldened to give you: the
Agrarian Co-operative Economy of the Provisional
Republic of Africa, the hope and destined fulfilment of the
Negro's dream. The New Africa shall stand before the

generations of tomorrow in final testimony of the black man's wisdom.' That's all.

LES. Papa. That's good!

DAN (*admiringly*). It's too bad you can't see anything but Garvey!

JUANITA. I'll say so.

VIC. I'm glad you like it. Get it together, Wanda – (*He joins her to lay aside his notes.*) Where's the children, Ella?

ELLA (*going to door*). Outside, somewhere.

DAN. The doubtfulness of your ever establishing the Republic aside – 'specially since Garvey's conviction – there's only one thing wrong with your conclusion.

ELLA (*in door, calling*). Caroline!

VIC (*to DAN*). Yeah – ?

ELLA (*to children*). You and Phillip come here – Papa's going!

VIC (*to DAN*). What's that?

DAN. You make the mistake of thinking the white man's idea of his superiority is something more than a delusion.

VIC. I was speaking about the effect of him having everything in the palm of his hand.

DAN. But that's temporary.

ELLA. Vic, you haven't got time to argue! (*She holds his jacket.*)

VIC (*starting to don it, but only succeeding in getting one arm in*). All I'm saying is, the white man's on top and he knows it, and as long as he stays on top all the books in the world won't change him.

DAN. There's more ways than one to skin a cat.

VIC. Yeah. Like what?

DAN. Use the white man's method, that's what – the process of individual achievement.

ELLA (*desperately, still trying to get him into his jacket*). Vic, it's pretty near train time.

MARTHA. They're goin' to keep on till they're hot at each other again!

VIC. Try offering your white man's method to the millions we got down South, living on cornbread and molasses and dying like flies from hookworm.

DAN (*sharply*). Let them –

JUANITA. Oh, cut it out, Dan? Vic's got to –

DAN. You shut up! (*To* VIC.) Why can't they come North, like we did? There's room up here for everybody!

VIC. Bunk. But even if there was, I'd still be against it.

DAN. Of course. Because you know it would put you race saviours out of business!

VIC (*losing his temper*). Yeah – well, there's one thing you can't deny: I'm against cutting my own brother's throat to get somewhere!

ELLA. For God's sake, Vic, stop it!

PHILLIP *and* CAROLINE *enter.*

DAN. The weak and shiftless always find some idea to blame for not having anything!

VIC. You're sitting pretty, ain't you?

DAN. I don't have to want for anything!

VIC. No you don't – living like a leech on the blood of your own people!

DAN. That's a lie!

JUANITA. Dan!

VIC. If it's a lie, how is it in a year you've been able to pay $4,000 for that automobile out there?

DAN. What's the matter, getting jealous?

VIC. For two cents I'd tell you what to do with that car!

DAN. Oh yes?

VIC. You're damn right! (*To* LES.) Go, call me a taxi!

LES *starts to obey, but is stopped by a glance from* ELLA.

MARTHA. I knowed it! I knowed it!

DAN (*going*). Come on, Juanita, to hell with him!

JUANITA. No, Dan! This is all uncalled for.

DAN. Like hell it is. You think I'm going to stand here and swallow his rotten insinuations?

ELLA. You're both acting like children.

VIC (*peremptorily, to* LES). Didn't I tell you to call me a taxi!

Exit LES, *running*.

JUANITA. You ought to be ashamed of yourself, Victor Mason. Two brother-in-laws arguing like cats and dogs.

VIC. You're wasting your breath!

JUANITA. Well, if that's the way you feel, goodbye!

She exits, with DAN.

MARTHA (*seeing* PHILLIP *with her work basket*). Phillip, you let that basket alone!

ELLA *dons her hat at hall-tree*.

VIC (*to* PHILLIP). Can't you keep out of mischief, boy?

PHILLIP (*pouting*). I wasn't doing nothing, Papa!

LES (*in door*). Here's the cab. (*He gets his father's bags*.)

VIC (*kissing* CAROLINE). Be a good girl, you hear. (*Turning to* PHILLIP.) Don't let your Ma have to give me any bad reports about you. (*Patting his shoulder*.) I'm going to try to bring you both something when I get back. (*To* WANDA.) Did you get it together?

She nods and hands him manuscript.

You've been a big help to me –

Kisses her forehead. Exit LES.

Take care of yourself.

He follows LES *out*.

Goodbye, Mama!

ELLA *goes out behind him*.

CAROLINE (*following her mother*). Mama, may I go to the
    station with you?

Exit CAROLINE.

PHILLIP (*on her heels*). Me, too, Mama?

Exit PHILLIP.

MARTHA *turns to the window as the curtain falls*.

Scene Two

The following January.

*From the window the light of the dreary winter dusk shrouds
the figure of* MARTHA, *who stands there, gazing into the
street.*

*This atmosphere of bleakness, in fact, pervades the whole
house and tends to emphasise the mood of the family, which is
one of apprehension and misgiving.*

ELLA *enters from above.*

ELLA (*halting on stairs*). Is it still snowing?

MARTHA (*immobile*). No. It's stopped.

ELLA (*strangely annoyed*). It would!

MARTHA (*turning*). If you'd made Vic keep that money, he
    wouldn't have to be shovellin' no snow – How is she?

ELLA (*turning to table to inspect punchbowl and cups there*).
    About the same. She drank the tea, but she's complaining
    about a headache.

MARTHA (*apprehensively*). You better call the doctor, then.
    She may be comin' down with the flu!

ELLA. I just spent the last nickel I had for the stuff to make
    the eggnog.

MARTHA (*sharply*). Lawd, Lawd! I don't know which one of
    you all is the worst, you or Vic.

ELLA. Oh, for heaven's sake, Mama! I can't have the leaders coming here to honour my own husband and not serve anything, can I?

MARTHA. If it was left to me, I'd serve 'em some water and give 'em a piece of my mind.

ELLA (*starting to kitchen*). If she isn't better by morning, I'll see Juanita – (*Halting and turning.*) Where's Phillip?

MARTHA. Outside.

ELLA (*astounded*). Outside – ! (*Upbraidingly*). Why didn't you make him stay in here?

MARTHA (*coldly*). I told him, but he's jes like his pappy!

ELLA (*crossing up to front door*). Lord have mercy! (*Opening door to call.*) Phillip! . . . You, Phillip!

PHILLIP (*in street*). Yes 'm!

ELLA (*angrily*). You come in this house! (*Shuts door and comes down.*) I don't know what I'm going to do with that boy.

MARTHA. Let him keep on runnin' round in the snow in them shoes and he'll be up there with Caroline, if you don't have to bury him!

PHILLIP (*entering*). Yes 'm? (*He wipes his nose with the back of his sleeve.*)

ELLA. Didn't Mama tell you to stay in this house?

PHILLIP. Mama, I wasn't doing nothin' but trying out Mac's new sled!

ELLA. I should try your backside! (*Pushing him into chair.*) Let me see those overshoes. (*Pulls off shoe.*) Just look at that hole!

MARTHA. I coulda told you a week ago. But I thought I better hold my tongue.

ELLA (*to* PHILLIP). Go upstairs and get in bed – (*As he does.*) And don't disturb Caroline . . . I'll bring you some hot eggnog in a little while.

On the stairs PHILLIP *sneezes.*

MARTHA. Phumph! Hear that?

ELLA *is silent as she goes to deposit* PHILLIP*'s shoes under hall-tree.*

ELLA (*glancing out of window*). It's snowing again, Thank God!

MARTHA *grunts.* ELLA *crosses to switch on lights.*

I reckon we'd better have a little light.

MARTHA (*seeing boy from window*). Here's Les 'n' Wanda.

She turns to greet him as he enters with his sister.

Gittin' colder, hunh?

LES *doffs his overcoat, as* WANDA *removes overshoes.*

LES. I don't think so, Grandma – (*Seeing punchbowl.*) Punchbowl out!

ELLA *remains preoccupied.*

MARTHA (*feigning surprise*). Oh, ain't you all heard? We's havin' a lil celebration this evening – your pappy's goin' be decorated!

WANDA. Decorated by whom? For what?

MARTHA. Ask your mammy – she knows all about it.

ELLA. I don't know myself. Only, Mr Strawder called up and said to keep your father home, as they were coming over to bestow some kind of honour on him. But, Wanda –

LES (*admiringly, as he enters kitchen*). Good old Papa.

WANDA. When's it coming off?

ELLA. I don't know. Mr Strawder just said they'll be here early.

WANDA (*going*). Well, I hope they come before I have to go.

ELLA (*intercepting her, hesitantly*). Wanda – you – have you – could you spare me a little money – a few dollars?

WANDA (*exploding wildly*). Money! Money! Can't you find anything else to speak to me about. I just gave you all I had payday! Where'd I get money from this time of the week?

ELLA. I wouldn't've asked you. But you know your father's still on strike – and Caroline's sick –

LES (*re-entering*). Caroline!

MARTHA. And Phillip, too!

WANDA. What's the matter with them?

ELLA. Caroline got her feet wet and the teacher sent her home.

MARTHA. For being ill-clad and needin' a doctor.

LES (*crossing to stairs*). Where are they – in bed?

ELLA. Yes.

As LES *runs upstairs:*

I'm not worrying about the doctor so much. But they both need overshoes.

WANDA (*going*). I'll see if I can get the boss to let me have a few dollars more tonight.

ELLA. Never mind. Maybe your father'll get hold of a dollar or two today.

Exit WANDA *upstairs.*

MARTHA (*warningly*). She goin' get tired of this money business pretty soon.

ELLA. Maybe it'll get a little easier for her. Vic said this morning he was going to ask Les to help.

MARTHA. Ask Les? How in the world's Les goin' do anything, and him goin' to college?

ELLA (*hearing stomping on porch*). I hate to think about it, but I reckon his father's going to make him drop out.

MARTHA. Lawdy! It's goin' break his heart!

ELLA *sees* VIC *enter, and measures him for a moment in silence.*

ELLA. Well, what'd you do today?

VIC *sets snow shovel down in corner and joins her, taking out change.*

VIC. Made six bits!

ELLA (*takes change to weigh it in palm*). Phump! – How long do you think we can keep this up?

VIC (*turning back to remove wraps*). I'm doing the best I can, Ella.

ELLA *goes out rear in silence*.

MARTHA (*shortly, watching him*). Do you know Caroline and Phillip's sick?

VIC (*shocked*). What the matter with them?

MARTHA. They got the flu, I 'spect.

VIC (*crossing and calling*). Ella! What's this about the children being sick?

ELLA (*offstage*). Take a look at their leaky shoes out there and you'll know for yourself.

VIC (*turning*). Their leaky shoes – ?

LES (*descending and catching sight of him*). Hello, Papa – I hear you're going to be decorated tonight.

VIC. What? What nonsense is this?

LES (*getting coat*). I've got to go by the kitchenette. But if they come, hold everything for me.

VIC (*as he starts out*). Wait a minute, son. There's something I wanted to ask you. (*Regretfully.*) I've been hoping to avoid it. But I reckon I needn't go into details. You see the hole I'm in –

LES. Yes . . . But what is it?

VIC. I guess there's no hope of my getting back to work before spring. So I thought I might ask you if you'd mind trying to help out with the house until times get better?

LES (*staggered*). But Papa – how?

VIC. Dan's paying you $10 a week, isn't he?

LES. Yes. But I need every cent for school. (*Suddenly understanding.*) You don't mean you want me to drop out – ?

VIC. I hate mighty bad to ask it, son –

LES. I see.

VIC. You'd only be out this quarter. By spring I'm sure I'll be back on the job –

LES (*going*). OK. Papa. I'll do it.

VIC. Thank you, son. You'll never regret it.

Exit LES. PERCY *enters from street, as* LES *passes him hurriedly.*

PERCY. Well! What's the matter with him?

VIC. Nothing. – How's things with you?

PERCY. Oh, I guess I'm still kicking – How're you, Mrs Brooks? (*He turns to hall-tree to doff wraps.*)

MARTHA. Pretty fair, I reckon.

VIC. Look, Percy, I wanted to ask if you could let me have a little money.

PERCY. A little money!

VIC. It looks like Phillip and Caroline've got the flu. So I thought if you could let me have about, say, a hundred dollars, to tide me over till spring. I'd be mighty much obliged to you.

PERCY (*staggered*). A hundred dollars! Captain, I ain't got the first quarter. Business at the hotel is shot to hell.

ELLA *enters and he nods to her.*

I'm not making enough to get by.

VIC (*sighing*). Well, I guess that settles it. (*Pause.*) I just thought I might be able to let Les stay in school.

PERCY. Is it that bad?

VIC. Couldn't be worse.

PERCY (*cynically*). I thought Wanda was doing all right!

ELLA (*catching note in his voice*). What you mean?

PERCY (*darkly*). Where's she?

ELLA (*eyeing him*). In her room, I guess.

PERCY. Where'd she get that fur coat?

ELLA. What fur coat?

PERCY. She's got a fur coat, hasn't she?

VIC. No. She's got a cloth coat.

PERCY. Just like I thought.

VIC. What do you mean, Percy?

PERCY. You've got trouble enough. But, for her sake, I guess I better tell you –

VIC. You mean Wanda's in some kind of trouble?

PERCY. I don't know. But I saw her in the Dreamland with a no-gooder last night, wearing a sealskin coat.

MARTHA (*incredulously*). A sealskin coat . . .

PERCY. Yep.

ELLA. You can't mean it!

PERCY. And if it didn't cost $500, it didn't cost a dime!

ELLA (*stunned*). Lord have mercy!

PERCY (*grimly*). I knew she was supposed to be taking care of the family. So . . . I figured it couldn't mean but one thing.

MARTHA. I been 'spectin' somethin' like this. (*To* ELLA.) I told you! I warned you!

ELLA (*striding to foot of stairs, calling*). Wanda!

WANDA (*above*). Yes! What is it?

ELLA. Come down here!

VIC. Maybe she borrowed it from somebody!

PERCY. Where're you going to find anybody dumb enough to take that kind of risk?

WANDA (*appearing above*). What is it, Mama?

ELLA (*abruptly, as she reaches floor*). Where's that sealskin coat you been wearing?

WANDA. What sealskin coat?

PERCY (*coldly*). The one you had on last night, that's what!

WANDA. Last night? (*She glances desperately around, trapped.*)

VIC. You did have one on, didn't you?

ELLA. And don't try to lie either, because Percy saw you!

WANDA (*concerned*). But Mama – Uncle Percy doesn't know what he's talking about –

VIC. Answer my question! Didn't you have one on last night?

WANDA (*after a moment*). Yes, I did.

ELLA. Where'd you get it?

WANDA. I bought it.

ELLA. You bought it? When? Where'd you get $500 to pay for it?

WANDA. It isn't paid for . . . I just got it out Christmas.

VIC. Well, where is it?

WANDA. Claudine's.

MARTHA. Sounds mighty fishy to me!

ELLA. What's it doing at Claudine's if you bought it?

WANDA. I've been leaving it there because I knew you'd kick about my having it.

ELLA. You're lying. You're lying as fast as you can open your mouth!

WANDA. I'm not. It's the truth!

ELLA. And I suppose you're going to try to tell me you've got receipts to show for it?

WANDA. Yes, I have.

VIC. Get them!

WANDA. I can't right now. They're over at Claudine's.

MARTHA. Phumn!

WANDA. Oh, I know what you're thinking. But it's true. I did buy that coat, and I've got the receipts to prove it!

ELLA. Well, you just get out of here and get them. And don't come back till you bring them, either.

WANDA *runs upstairs*.

MARTHA (*coldly*). Well, I reckon you'd better tell her goodbye, then!

VIC. I believe she's telling the truth.

MARTHA. If I was you, I wouldn't open mah mouth – you and Percy neither!

PERCY. What the hell did I have to do with it?

MARTHA (*accusingly*). She took after you, didn't she? If it hadn't been for you round here settin' her sich a bad example, she never would've started this 'goin' live' business – (*Sharply*.) Ella, if I was you, I'd bless him out, and Vic, too, right this minute –

She pauses, as WANDA *descends and goes out in silence*.

That gal's goin' make your heartache one of these days, sure's you're born!

Silence.

LES *re-enters*.

VIC (*turning to stairs*). I'm going get into my uniform before they come.

LES. What's the trouble, Mama?

ELLA. Nothing, nothing.

MARTHA. Here comes somebody.

LES. Not Mr Strawder and them?

He opens door to admit PISZER, *a young Jewish student, wearing a mackinaw and tam to match*.

LES. Piszer! This is a surprise! Come in!

PISZER (*warmly, in response to the other's friendliness*). Hello, Mason. I was on my way downtown, and I just thought I'd drop by to see if you'd care to go along?

LES. On a night like this? You're kidding. But come on in, I want you to meet my folks. Mom, this is Nathan Piszer, my classmate. Piszer, my mother.

ELLA. I'm very pleased to welcome you into our home.

PISZER (*shaking hands*). You're very cordial, Mrs Mason. Thank you.

LES. My grandmother, Mrs Brooks –

MARTHA (*shaking hands*). I'm pleased to meet you.

LES. And my uncle, Mr Mason –

PERCY (*shaking hands*). How do you do?

LES. Give me your coat, and sit down.

ELLA. Yes, do, Mr Piszer. You're no stranger here. Les has talked so much about you, we all feel we know you.

PISZER. Thank you, Mrs Mason. But seriously, I can't stay. (*Turning to* LES.) I'm on my way down to Orchestra Hall, and I thought perhaps you might like to go along – Some Van Gorham is lecturing on Russia, and they say he's a pretty keen observer.

LES. Gee, I'd like to. But I'm afraid I can't tonight. You see, we're holding a little celebration for my dad, and –

PISZER. Is that so? Then I'm probably intruding –

LES. No, no! Not at all. We'd like you to stay, wouldn't we, Mama?

ELLA. Yes, you must, Mr Piszer.

LES (*pressing him*). I want you to meet my dad –

PISZER. I'd like to –

LES. Good. Give me your coat.

PISZER (*doffing coat*). But why're you honouring him?

LES (*laughing*). You've got me there! You see, he's one of the local leaders of the Garvey Movement, and I guess it's a sort of surprise. (*He takes coat.*)

PISZER (*following him*). The Garvey Movement – ? I'd no idea your folks were connected with it. If you don't mind me saying, isn't it –

ELLA (*going*). You must excuse me, Mr Piszer. But I must get into the kitchen – Come on, Mama, and fix Phillip's eggnog.

MARTHA. I'm so sorry to leave you, Mr Piszer.

She exits with ELLA.

LES (*offering* PISZER *chair*). Go on, Piszer.

PISZER. Well, frankly, isn't the movement really just a pipe dream?

LES. Hunh? There's nothing impractical about it. There's no hope for my race in this country, so any programme that offers escape is all right with me. How about you, Uncle Percy?

PERCY. Of course, Les. But you can't expect him to see it like we do.

PISZER. I don't know, Mr Mason. There may be another solution.

LES. And?

PISZER. The lasting solution for minority groups today is unity with the majority on a common ground.

LES *laughs*.

You're sceptical – ?

PERCY. As a Jew, can you blame him?

LES. Nothing could be more of a pipe dream than that.

PISZER. It may sound remote. But what's there to prevent all the underprivileged from getting together?

LES (*bitterly*). The same that makes them call you 'Sheeny' and me 'Nigger'.

PERCY. All this interracial conciliation is nothing but a trap to catch the Negro in!

PISZER. But I'm thinking of socialism.

LES (*laughing*). What? Don't tell me you've gone Bolshevik?

PISZER. Have you read Lenin?

LES (*subsiding*). No – have you?

PISZER. Yeah. Perhaps –

MARTHA (*crossing with eggnog*). 'Scuse passin', Les. I got to get upstairs to mah sick.

There is a loud knocking and stomping out front.

LES (*springing up, and going to door*). Oh, hello, Mr Strawder. Come on in, you all! (*Calling.*) Mam! Here's Mr Strawder and them!

STRAWDER *and* COTTON *enter doffing their overcoats to reveal the splendour of their regalia – coloured sashes above their black, red-striped uniforms – and a woman,* SISTER GABRELLA, *in white with a black cross on her sleeve, the insignia of the Black Cross Nurses of the Movement.*

STRAWDER. Where's Brother Mason? Where is the Captain?

ELLA (*entering with pot of steaming eggnog*). He's upstairs. I've made some eggnog to warm you up!

COTTON. Just what we need on a night like this!

STRAWDER *sees* VIC *descend with* MARTHA *behind him.*

STRAWDER (*commandingly*). Good evening, Brother Mason. Brother Mason, it is my great privilege and honour to greet you on this occasion, and to convey to you the sentiments of our president. (*He pauses dramatically.*) For your paper on the Future of Co-operative Farming in Africa that you read at the Negro World Conference, our leader has commanded me to greet you with the title of Lord of Agriculture of the Provisional Republic of Africa –

Everyone cheers.

Quiet. Let me finish before you start celebrating.

PHILLIP *and* CAROLINE *creep down on stairs to peep through the banister.*

Sister Gabrella!

SISTER GABRELLA *steps forward with long red sash, which she places on* VIC.

PHILLIP. Look at Papa!

STRAWDER. Friends and Brothers of the UNIA, we honour here the man who put us on the map and set our banner

flying before the eyes of all our black brothers. And now,
My Lord, I duly bestow upon you this emblem of your rank!

The group cheers as STRAWDER *pins on a medallion.*

ALL. Speech! Speech!

VIC (*lifting his hand for silence*). Brothers and Sister, I thank
you for this display of affection. And I appreciate this great
honour. But I feel I ought to call your attention to the way
I think about what I've done . . . I only prepared and read
a paper . . . and none of the things it deals with have been
accomplished. We're still in the hands of the enemy with
our children cut off from opportunity, and the lynch rope
lying ready for any black man who dares to raise his head.
We have yet, my friends, to acquire a single inch of the soil
of Africa that we can call our own. And while we celebrate,
our leader stands within the shadow of the penitentiary,
branded as a common criminal . . . These are dark and
terrible truths, my friends, and as I face them, I feel – well,
I ask you to drink a pledge with me. (*Lifting cup, which is
handed him.*) Brothers and Sister, and members of my
family, let us pledge our hearts and minds and the last
ounce of our strength to carry on without ceasing, until our
cause is won, and the black man has achieved his place in
the God-given sun: a free man, honoured and respected in
the eyes of the nations of the world!

The silence is eloquent, as they all drink.

STRAWDER (*shaking hands*). My Lord, that was a speech to
be proud of.

COTTON. Yes, sir!

VIC. Thank you, Count! Both of you.

STRAWDER. I'm sorry we ain't got time to stay a while, but
we've got two more promotions to take care of.

He leads the way out.

COTTON. See you Sunday.

They exit.

LES. Papa, this is my classmate, Nathan Piszer –

He draws PISZER *forward.*

VIC. I'm glad to know you, son.

PISZER. Your speech was very moving.

VIC. Thank you. (*To* ELLA.) And I'm mighty much obliged to you, Ella, for the eggnog – (*Taking bowl away from her.*) Let me take it. (*He takes bowl into kitchen.*)

PISZER (*getting his coat*). I guess I'll beat it – I think I've still time to make Van Gorham's lecture.

LES (*getting his own coat*). I'll go with you – it's early yet.

ELLA. You must come back and see us again, Mr Piszer.

PISZER. Thank you, I shall, Mrs Mason.

> ELLA *and* VIC *shake hands with him.*

Goodbye!

> PISZER *and* LES *exit.* VIC *is re-entering.*

PERCY (*to* VIC). I guess I'll be running on myself, Vic.

VIC. Have you had supper?

PERCY. No. But I don't want nothing. I've got to see about getting me a drink. (*He dons his overcoat.*)

ELLA. Come on, Mama, if you're going to eat.

> *She starts back into kitchen, but the front door opens and* DAN *enters.*

DAN. Say, Vic. What do you mean by taking that boy out of school?

VIC (*annoyed*). Now hold your horses. Lester Mason happens to be my son!

DAN. So what? I'm responsible for him being in school.

VIC. I grant you that. But you can be civil about it –

DAN. You've got a nerve!

VIC. Never mind. In the first place, it's only temporary. I just asked him to sacrifice going back this quarter.

DAN. What right've you got to demand such a sacrifice?

VIC. I'd rather not discuss this.

DAN. Oh, you wouldn't? Well, let me tell you this: I'm not paying Les to support you. Not by a damn sight!

PERCY. I wouldn't take that attitude, Dan. Put yourself in his place. The children are upstairs sick in bed, and you know how far the little money Wanda's been making goes –

VIC. Never mind, Percy. Let him go on. He's been waiting for a chance to rub it in.

DAN (*surprised*). I'm not trying to rub anything –

VIC. Actions speak louder than words. You know I'm up against it. You know I've been up against it for months.

DAN. I'm not offering my money to anyone who's too proud to ask for it.

VIC. So you want me to come crawling to you, eh?

PERCY. Yeah, so he can lord it over you!

DAN. Lord, hell! You're both just jealous of my success. But to show you there's nothing cheap about me, I tell you what I'll do. I'll let you have enough money to see you through –

PERCY (*surprised*). No!

DAN. That is, if you're willing to give up this foolish Garvey business and act like you've got some sense.

VIC. What exactly do you mean?

DAN. I'll let you have two or three hundred dollars, if you'll turn over that Black Star Line stock.

ELLA. Dan, you don't mean it?

VIC. As collateral?

DAN. Collateral, hell! What kind of businessman do you think I am?

VIC. You'd sell it, then?

DAN. Of course. Maybe I can find enough suckers to take it at a third its face value.

VIC. Phumph! Big-hearted Dan – forget it. I can't do it.

DAN. No. You'd rather frustrate the life of your son while you hang on to your silly dream!

VIC. Call it what you like. At my age a man can't look forward to carrying a hod for the rest of this life.

DAN. At your age a man should be thinking about the future of his children.

VIC. That's just it. What kind of future have they? Aren't we still in the hands of the enemy, browbeaten, stigmatised . . . But what's the use – if you want to lend me a little money, all right. I'll appreciate it and pay you back, if it takes me till my dying day. But don't ask me to part with my stock.

LES *enters*.

DAN. Business is business – Ella, you see my point, don't you?

ELLA. Yes, I do – give it to him, Vic. Take the money. It can't hurt Garvey. It will only be a matter of it changing hands –

VIC. Ella, that stock's worth $1,500, have you forgotten that?

ELLA. It won't be worth a dime if Caroline needs a doctor!

PERCY (*supporting her*). A smart flea, Captain, knows when to hop!

VIC. I've had my say.

ELLA. Yes, you have. But I haven't had mine. I'm getting sick to death of this scrimping and worrying and waiting from day to day for something that never comes. (*Furiously.*) Do you know the rent hasn't been paid yet? That we hardly got bread to eat in this house? That the children need shoes?

VIC. It's no use getting hot, Ella. I know all that. It's the lot of every black man in the country. But it's a mighty poor slave that gives up trying to break his chains just because there's a nick in the hammer!

DAN (*going*). OK, Captain. If you're going to remain a fool, hang on to your stock. I'm not going to argue with you all night. I'm going. But get this through your head: you needn't expect a dime from me as long as you do. (*Exits.*)

ELLA. Wait, Dan – (*Desperately.*) Call him back, Vic. Call him back!

Curtain.

Scene Three

Early evening, a month later.

The atmosphere remains the same, a dreariness hanging over everything like a pall, seeming to penetrate through the window from the sooty snow-laden street, as PHILLIP *sits there looking out.* CAROLINE *is lying on the couch beneath a quilt, with her grandmother beside her, whom she is watching as she dresses a black doll.*

CAROLINE (*after a moment*). That's not right, Grandma!

> MARTHA *tosses the doll in* CAROLINE'*s lap with an impatient thrust, then rises.*

MARTHA. Here, you take this black thing! I don't want no more to do with it!

> PHILLIP *darts a glance at her, and simultaneously kicks the rocker in an automatic, vicious reflex.*

Are you trying to break that chair? What's the matter with you? (*Guiltily.*) You act like you crazy.

> PHILLIP *rises abruptly and crosses to the Victrola, where he sulks as* MARTHA *goes on.*

(*Complainingly.*) I never seen sich chillun for gittin' on a person's nerves!

> *There is a sound of stomping on the porch.* LES *enters as they all turn to look.*

LES. Phew!

> *He closes the door behind him and lows his breath into his fists, flapping his armpits.*

(*To* PHILLIP.) You're lucky you didn't have to go to school today!

MARTHA. How cold is it now?

LES (*hanging his coat up*). About ten below, I guess.

> *He goes upstairs.* ELLA *appears from rear.*

ELLA. Was that Les?

CAROLINE. Yes 'm.

ELLA (*seeing* PHILLIP *in corner*). What're you doing, sulking over there?

PHILLIP (*dully*). Nothing.

ELLA *eyes him questioningly.* VIC *descends the stairs.*

MARTHA. Dinner 'bout ready?

ELLA. Just about.

VIC. Anybody seen the paper?

ELLA (*turning to go*). There isn't any paper.

VIC (*annoyed, going to window*). There isn't? I'm going to write in about that boy!

ELLA. You'd do better paying him?

VIC (*turning in surprise*). You haven't paid him?

ELLA. What was I going to pay him with?

VIC. It ain't but fifteen cents a week! I can't see –

ELLA (*going, angrily*). Is that so? Well, hereafter you see he gets it!

She exits to rear.

VIC. Phumph!

WANDA *enters from the street, in tears and shivering.*

Now what's the matter with you? And where's your coat?

LES *descends.*

WANDA (*sobbing*). They took it!

MARTHA. Who took it?

LES. Wanda?

WANDA. The Sheriff.

MARTHA. The Sheriff! (*Shouting.*) Ella!

VIC (*amazed*). But how?

WANDA (*extending paper*). He just took it with this.

VIC (*joining her*). What is it?

ELLA (*entering*). What's the matter?

MARTHA. The Sheriff's done had a-hold of Wanda. Done took that sealskin coat off her!

VIC (*to* WANDA). How many payments do you owe?

WANDA. Only seven.

VIC. Seven – that's $35. (*Shaking his head, helplessly.*) Lord, Lord! –

ELLA. More good money burnt up!

WANDA *bursts into tears anew and runs upstairs.*

LES. But Papa, she practically owns the coat!

VIC. What does the law care?

MARTHA. She had no business buyin' it!

DAN, *swaddled in an expensive grey ulster, enters.*

VIC. What brings you here on a night like this?

DAN. Then you haven't heard – ?

VIC. Heard what?

DAN. The news about Garvey.

VIC. No. What about him?

DAN. They took him to Atlanta today, that's what!

VIC (*staggered*). What?

DAN. I told you that monkey-chaser was no good!

VIC. But the Supreme Court – ?

DAN. Denied his appeal, they took him into custody this morning.

VIC (*sitting with an air of defeat*). Well, sir!

ELLA (*sympathetically*). Don't take it so hard, Vic, it's no more than you expected.

VIC. I guess you're right. He was framed from the start.

MARTHA. Les, I thought you told me Marcus Garvey confessed 'bout that money?

LES (*hesitantly*). Well, he did, Grandma. But not –

DAN. You bet he did. He's as guilty as hell. I tried to tell you.

ELLA (*ominously*). If you've come to crow over us, you can get out!

DAN. Hold on, Ella. I feel as bad over this as you do. But you know we couldn't tell him nothing. Hell, the truth is the truth!

VIC (*rising*). Yeah. And if it was big as the Woolworth Building you wouldn't see it.

DAN. Why in the hell don't you wake up? Your movement's dead as a mackerel!

VIC (*angrily*). Why do you persist in meddling in my affairs?

DAN (*backing away*). OK, OK, big shot. (*Going.*) But you mark my word: with that monkey-chaser in jail, your $1,500 is burnt up, and your movement's going to peter out to nothing.

He exits.

ELLA. You'd better come and get your dinner, Vic. (*To* PHILLIP.) Go set the table.

Exit PHILLIP.

VIC. No, Ella. You all go ahead. I'm going up and lie down for a while.

LES (*as his father turns to go*). I'm sorry, Papa.

VIC. No man is indispensable. We'll carry on.

Exit LES.

ELLA. If you don't mind, Vic. Take Caroline up to bed. She's been down here too long already –

To CAROLINE, *as* VIC *bears her away.*

I'll bring you some soup in a little while.

VIC (*carrying* CAROLINE *above*). How do you feel?

CAROLINE. All right.

Exit VIC *and* CAROLINE.

ELLA (*seeing her mother trying to thread needle*). Give it to me, Mama.

MARTHA (*as* ELLA *threads it*). Well, it looks like Dan was right after all –

ELLA. Mama, I'm in no mood.

MARTHA. No. I reckon not. (*She rummages through her work basket.*) Now, where's my sizzers? (*Angrily.*) Ain't nobody tetched them sizzers but Phillip. (*Rising to call.*) Phillip!

PHILLIP (*in rear*). Yes 'm!

MARTHA (*crossing*). Where's my sizzers?

PHILLIP (*in rear*). I don't know, Grandma. I ain't seen 'em!

MARTHA (*rushing out*). You ain't, hunh? . . . You stinkin' rascal!

There is an outburst from PHILLIP.

Didn't I tell you not to bother my sizzers!

ELLA (*crossing, her voice rising above the shouts of the child*). Turn him loose, Mama! Turn him loose!

The cries of the child subside, and MARTHA *re-enters in a huff, out of breath.*

Lord, Mama, I don't know what I'm going to do about you. I told you if you want any of the children whipped to call me or Vic. You can't be wrestling with that boy! The first thing you know you'll fall and knock your head against something!

PHILLIP *enters meanwhile, sulking as he glares at his grandmother.*

MARTHA (*angrily*). You don't have to beat 'round the stump! (*Shaking her finger at* PHILLIP.) If you don't want me to put mah hands on that black scamp, why don't you say so?

ELLA (*angrily*). Mama, I've asked you not to call that boy black where he can hear you!

MARTHA. Yes, he's black. Black like his cranky daddy!

ELLA. Don't mind her, Phillip – go upstairs and sit with Caroline till I call you.

PHILLIP *ascends stairs and disappears.*

MARTHA. I know when my bread is brown. (*Going out rear.*) I'm goin' git my few rags and git outta here. That's what I'm goin' do!

She exits to rear.

ELLA (*crossing to rear door*). Oh, yeah? And where do you think you're going to find a place to stay – Juanita's?

MARTHA (*offstage*). Yes, Juanita's! She'll give me a place to lay mah weary head.

ELLA. She will, hunh?!

MARTHA (*entering with armful of clothing*). Don't you fool yourself. Don' you do it. Juanita's got Dupree blood in her veins! (*She dumps the garments on couch.*)

ELLA. You and your Dupree blood! You want to get over to Dan's where you think you won't suffer – !

MARTHA. That's a lie!

ELLA (*furiously*). For nearly ten years this house has been good enough for you. But now you think we're on the breadline, you want to save your own skin. You want to get over there where you think you'll be safe!

MARTHA. That's another lie! 'Tain't no sich!

VIC *appears above, buttoning his jacket. But* MARTHA *doesn't see him.*

You's jes making that up outta jealousy, like that evil, black, good-for-nothin' nigger you call your husband!

VIC (*woundedly*). So!

ELLA (*glancing up, frightened*). Vic!

MARTHA, *realising she has committed the unpardonable sin in interracial relations, backs up, full of guilt and fear.*

VIC (*coming down, his voice cold and hostile*). So I'm an evil, black, good-for-nothing nigger!

ELLA (*joining him, anxiously*). For God's sake, Vic. Overlook
it!

VIC (*to* MARTHA, *as she stands at bay*). What've I ever done
to make you say such a harsh thing about me?

ELLA (*soothingly*). Nothing, Vic. And she knows it.

MARTHA (*in belligerent fear*). Don't you put no words in
mah mouth! I ain't scared of him and nobody like him.

ELLA (*shouting*). Will you shut up!

MARTHA. Don't you tell me to shut up! Don't you do it!

ELLA (*turning to* VIC). Don't pay her no mind, Vic. She's just
upset – excited because I got after her about whipping
Phillip!

VIC. You needn't try to cover up for her, Ella. I've stumbled
into something and you know it.

ELLA. She's just imagining things –

VIC. Like calling me the dirtiest thing she can think of?

ELLA. Don't get off on the wrong track, Vic. What she said
she said out of anger with me. And if you hadn't come
down here so quietly you never would've heard her.

VIC. What am I supposed to do, blow a trumpet every time
I move in my own house?

ELLA. No, Vic. Of course not. I only meant –

VIC (*to* MARTHA, *coldly*). I'm too black for your Dupree
blood, isn't that it?

MARTHA (*venomously*). The cap must fit you or you wouldn't
be wearing it!

ELLA (*pained*). Oh, Mama!

VIC. You miserable old hypocrite.

MARTHA. Well, there's one thing. I ain't never been no
hypocrite with you!

ELLA. Lord, Mama. You ought to be ashamed of yourself!

MARTHA. Shame, nothin'. I ain't got nothin' to be shamed of.

VIC (*coldly*). No. But you let this sink into your twisted soul –
you don't hate me. You envy me. You envy my black skin
because in your heart, you know yours is nothing but a
badge of shame!

ELLA (*gasping*). Oh, God!

MARTHA. Ella, you goin' stand there and let him insult me
like that?

ELLA (*to* VIC). Please, Vic, could she help it if she was born
out of wedlock?

VIC. No. What I resent is the cheap dishonesty of her attitude.
She's got nothing against me, and she knows it. But she's
like the rest of her kind, who let the colour of their skin
drive them to think black people are some kind of dirt
beneath their feet, when nothing could be more idiotic than
the pride they take in the blood of their raping ancestors!

MARTHA. You hear that, Ella? (*Crying in outrage, as she
gathers clothing.*) To think the day would ever come when
anybody'd say sich things bout me! But I'll git you. I'll git
even with you, you black viper, if it's the last thing I do!
(*Going to door and turning with parting shot.*) You'll see if
I don't!

She exits.

ELLA (*stunned*). If anybody had told me you could be so low
down, I'd've spit on them!

VIC (*quietly*). The truth always seem ugly when it's hard to
look at.

ELLA. It serves me right. I should've listened years ago.

VIC. Just what do you mean by that?

ELLA. Don't ask me what I mean. Don't ask me nothing.

VIC. Ella –

ELLA (*venomously*). I despise you!

VIC. Ella, for God's sake, don't –

ELLA. Yes, I despise you. You hear me? I despise you! And I
think you're everything Mama said and then some.

VIC. You don't mean that, Ella. You can't mean it.

ELLA. I don't, huh? What do I have to say to make you know it?

VIC. Nothing, Ella, you're hurt. But God knows I had no intention of hurting you. (*Distraught.*) I guess the news about Garvey, then this, just about floored me. But you must know I meant no offence to you. I ask your pardon.

ELLA. You can keep your apologies. I don't want them. For twenty years I've let you treat me like a doormat and run things to suit yourself. And now you've got the nerve to insult my mother right before my face. (*Raving.*) Who do you think you are, King Jesus?

VIC (*quietly*). I've always considered you, Ella.

ELLA. You let Wanda quit school against my wishes! Who else but you and your fool ideas started her on the road to hell? And this Garvey business. Where's all the money I helped you save? (*In sudden tears.*) Whose fault is it I can't stop a bread wagon to feed my children?

VIC. So you blame me for the world?

ELLA (*ignoring him*). I've been a woman and a wife to you. But I'm through with you! You hear me? I'm through with you!

VIC. You can't mean that, Ella. You wouldn't leave me?

ELLA. No. But I can make you wish I would! If it wasn't for Caroline and the rest, I'd follow Mama out of this house and never put my feet back in it again!

VIC. I'll get out if you want me to.

ELLA (*going*). Suit yourself. Get out or stay! Or better still, go on to Africa. Maybe you'll find the company of your own kind in the jungle!

She exits above.

VIC, *wounded, moves down to bang the back of the chair beside the couch.*

VIC. Prejudice! Everywhere you turn, nothing but prejudice. A black man can't even get away from it in his own house!

(*Overwhelmed by the irony, he emits a prolonged sound.*)
Phummmmnnh! Phummmmnnh! Phummmmnnh!

Impelled by the onslaught of pain, he recognises the very essence of his oppression.

And like a fool I dreamed of getting away from it in Africa!

Slowly he sinks into the chair, as the curtain falls.

ACT THREE

Scene One

Early August, 1932. A late afternoon.

Ostensibly the living room has not changed. Its furnishings are the same, but there is no longer the brightness and orderliness that characterised it before. Now everywhere is manifest some sign of the family's desperate impoverishment, as it continues its struggle in the midst of the general breakdown of the nation's economy, the Great Depression.

Present are ELLA, *wearing a frayed apron and the aspect of care;* WANDA, *in a good skirt and sweater of light material, indicative of her continued capacity to earn a living; and* MARKS, *a Jewish used-furniture dealer, in an old suit. A man of fifty-odd years with eloquent gestures, he is seemingly at the end of his wits in the effort to strike a bargain.*

MARKS. Sell! Sell! Everybody wants to sell. But nobody wants to buy. Can I help it if everybody wants to sell, Mrs Mason, and nobody wants to buy? Maybe you didn't hear there's a depression – ?

ELLA (*stubbornly*). But, Mr Marks, you can give me more than $3 for that couch. I paid $79 for it!

MARKS (*with a quick, snapping glance at couch*). You should pay $79 for such a couch – Oh, moi, come on, I'll make it $3.50.

WANDA (*outraged*). $3.50!

MARKS (*confidingly*). To anybody else I wouldn't pay half so much.

ELLA. I wouldn't think of it.

MARKS. Maybe I should keep it a whole year and can't sell it to nobody!

WANDA. Oh sure!

ELLA (*indicating machine*). Well, what'll you give me for that Victrola?

MARKS (*throwing up his hands*). The Victrola you couldn't give me!

WANDA. Oh, no – ?

MARKS (*annoyed by her sarcasm*). Listen, lady. Business is bad – you know that? Nobody wants to buy a Victrola. Nobody wants to buy anything. (*To* ELLA.) Well, what you say?

ELLA (*indicating chair centre*). What about that chair – ?

MARKS (*examining chair, slowly*). The chair, it isn't so good. But . . . maybe with the chair and couch together I could give you $5.

WANDA (*angrily*). Tell him to go to hell, Mama!

MARKS. What's the matter with you? I offer Mrs Mason the top price, and you tell me to go to hell! You think I got no feelings? I'm a man with a family. You want me to ruin myself?

WANDA. Swell chance you've got to ruin yourself!

MARKS (*turning to* ELLA). Well, what you say? You want to sell?

ELLA (*dejectedly*). No. Never mind. I just thought I could raise a few dollars to help me get another place. But the little you offer won't do us any good.

MARKS (*sympathetically*). Times are bad, Mrs Mason. But you won't find anybody'll give you more, even if you should search the city over.

ELLA (*bitterly*). I'd rather put them in the stove! (*She wipes her eyes.*)

WANDA. Don't, Mama.

MARKS. Come, I'll give you $6.

WANDA. Big-hearted Mr Marks!

ELLA (*desperately*). Make it $10 and you can have them.

WANDA. No, Mama. No!

MARKS. I should make it $10? Why, I could buy a finer couch and chair for $5. (*He starts out.*) You don't want to do business, Mrs Mason.

ELLA. Take them for $8.

MARKS (*with finality*). I'll give you $6.50 and no more!

ELLA (*breaking*). I'll chop them to pieces first!

WANDA (*furiously*). You get out of here! You – you – you're a disgrace to your race!

MARKS (*backing out*). All right, all right, lady! Don't get sore!

He bumps into CLAUDINE *as he starts to exit. She is in a summer frock and looking quite chic.*

CLAUDINE. Hey! Why don't you look where you're going?

MARKS (*disappearing*). Excuse me, please.

Exit MARKS.

WANDA (*half-heartedly greeting* CLAUDINE). Hello, Claudine.

CLAUDINE (*noticing* ELLA). What's the matter?

WANDA (*embarrassed*). Don't cry, Mama. Everything's going to be all right. You go upstairs and lie down for a while and quiet your nerves.

CLAUDINE (*sympathetically*). Is there anything I can do for you, Mrs Mason?

ELLA. No, Claudine. I guess I'll just have to let them set us out, and make the best of it. (*She climbs stairs in tears.*)

CLAUDINE. You all going to be evicted, too, hunh?

WANDA. I guess so. Papa's gone to court now.

CLAUDINE. Well, that's too bad! But it's your own fault!

WANDA. Where do you get that stuff – it's my fault?

CLAUDINE. If you had any sense you wouldn't be in this trouble.

WANDA. Oh yeah?

CLAUDINE. You're damn right! (*She lights a cigarette*.) I wish I could get a break with an old chump like Hogan. I'd take his sugar so quick, he'd think I was a gangster!

WANDA. I've told you, I don't go for that!

CLAUDINE. No, you're too dumb. Here you are with your Mama about to be set out in the street, and all you've got to do is ask that old sucker for the money to save her.

WANDA. I know. I know. But I just can't bring myself round to it.

CLAUDINE. Baloney! Crazy as Hogan is about you, all you have to do is ask him for the dough.

WANDA. I know. In fact, I already have.

CLAUDINE (*surprised*). You have? Then you've got more sense than I gave you credit for!

WANDA. I just thought I'd ask him last night to see what he'd say.

CLAUDINE. Sweet potatoes! And he shelled right out, didn't he?

WANDA. No. There's a catch in it. He wanted me to promise to be nice to him – I can't stomach that!

CLAUDINE. Don't talk foolish, Wanda. There won't be nothing to it. Hogan's not so bad. He's just old. Anyway – (*Going to table for an ashtray*.) you're no virgin, you know!

WANDA (*sharply*). No. But I'm no whore!

CLAUDINE (*snuffing cigarette*). You're a fool, if you ask me. But she's your mother, kiddo. If you don't care whether she's set out in disgrace before all the neighbours, it's your lookout. But I'll tell you one thing: you'd never catch me turning my mother down for the sake of such a flimsy idea. (*Going*.) But I've got to get home. You'd better think it over like you got some sense.

She exits.

WANDA (*contemplatively*). Think it over – (*She shudders*.) God!

She buries her face in the palms of her hands and is lost until she hears ELLA *descending.*

I thought you were going to lie down for a while?

ELLA. My pillow's like a bag of rocks . . . Claudine gone?

WANDA. Yes.

ELLA. Isn't it time for you to be going to work?

WANDA. What time is it?

ELLA. My clock had 5.30. But I wouldn't trust it.

WANDA (*preoccupied, still sitting*). I guess I'd better get ready.

ELLA. I guess you'd better.

DAN *appears – seedily dressed and bereft of his former cocksureness – accompanied by* LES, *in sweatshirt and trousers.*

DAN. Well, what'd they do? (*He sits.*)

ELLA. I don't know. Vic's still downtown.

LES (*noticing his mother's eyes*). You've been crying.

WANDA. Marks upset her.

LES. Marks? What Marks?

WANDA. The furniture man. You should've heard what he offered her for that couch and chair – $6.50!

She goes above.

DAN. Can you beat it? But it's no more than you can expect from a Jew!

LES. That's prejudice, Uncle Dan.

DAN. Call it what you like. But I'm sick of them – they're all alike!

LES. The white man says the same thing about us. But the Jews are no different from any other people. If anything, they've contributed a damn sight more.

DAN. Oh, yeah – another of your Communistic ideas, eh?

LES. It didn't take the Communists to find that out.

He sits. CAROLINE *enters, now a fine-looking girl of twenty-two, neatly dressed.*

ELLA (*coldly*). For God's sake, let the Jews rest! (*Seeing* CAROLINE.) I thought you went to Juanita's?

CAROLINE (*pretending to search for mail on table*). I just left her.

ELLA (*suspiciously*). You didn't stay long.

CAROLINE (*glancing at* DAN, *who squirms*). I can't understand her any more, Mama. She acts so funny.

DAN. What was she doing?

ELLA. What do you mean, she acts funny?

LES *is smiling, apparently enjoying* DAN*'s predicament.*

CAROLINE (*glancing at* LES). Oh, I don't know, Mama. Did Papa get back?

ELLA (*persisting*). It's mighty strange you can't explain what you mean –

CAROLINE *is studiously avoiding* DAN, *who has inched toward the edge of his chair. She goes to couch.*

CAROLINE. Every time I go there lately she watches me and Grandma like a hawk.

DAN (*uneasily*). That's just your imagination.

CAROLINE. Maybe so. But she made me feel like I was in the way. I just told her goodbye and came home. (*She reads.*)

DAN (*defensively*). Juanita's just worried like everybody else.

ELLA (*after a moment*). I wish your father would come on!

LES. The courts are packed, Mama. They're evicting right and left.

DAN (*relieved at turn of conversation*). They have to protect people's property and to hell with the people!

ELLA. For fifteen years Cochran never missed a month getting his rent on this house.

DAN. Sure. But what can you expect when nine out of ten tenants are nothing but deadbeats?

LES. That's a lot of hooey. If the big dogs can't give us work, they've no right to expect any rent. A just government would make them bear their part of the responsibility.

DAN (*bitterly*). Yeah. I bore my part and see what it got me!

LES. It serves you right for kidding yourself.

DAN. Oh yeah?

LES. You doggone tooting! You've never been anything but a Negro striver, trying to go big. And now, even though you've been wiped out, you still can't see what hit you!

DAN (*angrily*). You rattle-brained, young snipe! If you weren't my own nephew – !

ELLA. Dan, is that necessary?

LES. Don't mind him, Mama.

ELLA. We've all made mistakes –

DAN. Mistake nothing. Suppose I'd a-kept my money in the bank, would I have it?

LES. Just another contradiction in the present rotten order.

DAN. You wise punk! You're just like your daddy –

ELLA (*exploding*). Oh, stop it! I'm sick of listening to nothing but talk, talk! For twenty years that's all we've had in this family – ain't nobody done nothing yet!

DAN (*rising*). I guess you're right, Ella. (*Joining* LES.) Gimme a cigarette.

LES. I can't afford them.

DAN (*going*). Well, maybe you reds'll include them in the rations when you get in power.

LES *smiles*.

(*Turning to* ELLA.) I'll be back, Ella. I'm just going to the corner.

He exits through front door.

ELLA (*going*). I guess I'll go put the little we got on the stove.

She exits into rear.

CAROLINE. I think you're foolish to argue with him, Les.

WANDA *descends with purse.*

LES (*rising, his eyes on* WANDA). I've been waiting for a chance to see you.

WANDA (*going to front door*). Yeah. Well, you'll have to do it later.

LES (*intercepting her*). I said I wanted to talk to you, and I don't mean tomorrow. Excuse us, will you, Caroline?

CAROLINE (*going*). Of course . . .

WANDA. But I've got to get to the drugstore.

LES. I can't help that – sit down.

WANDA. I won't sit down. You can't bully me.

LES. Mama's in the kitchen. Perhaps, you'd rather I spoke to her?

WANDA. What'd you mean?

LES. You know what I mean.

WANDA. You haven't got anything on me!

LES. No? Sit down and keep your voice low.

WANDA (*hesitates, measuring him for a moment, then sits*). All right.

LES turns away in silence, and takes a stride or two, apparently gathering his thoughts.

Well, why don't you say what you're going to say?

LES. I don't suppose you realise it, Wanda. But it's been pretty painful to Papa and me, sitting round here day after day, allowing you to bear the burden of the house –

WANDA. When have you heard me complaining?

LES. Never. But it's begun to look as if it's about to get you down, isn't that so?

WANDA. No. Who said it was?

LES. Nobody. But the facts seem to indicate it.

WANDA. Come to the point.

LES. All right. I will. I saw you get out of that car around the corner last night.

WANDA. You what – ?

LES. You're slipping!

WANDA. But it was nothing like that, Les. Honest. He was just an old drug salesman who always comes into the store.

LES. Then why didn't you let him bring you to the door?

WANDA (*truthfully*). Because I knew you or some of the rest would misunderstand – that's why!

LES (*quietly*). Don't lie, Wanda. You're a grown woman, and you don't have to tell me anything. (*His voice fills with bitter irony.*) But you know damn well, when a white man begins to take a 'nigger girl' riding, it can't mean but one thing!

WANDA. But you're wrong!

LES. I'm not. You're trifling with him. – (*He presses.*) Aren't you?

WANDA. No! No!

LES. I say you are!

WANDA (*outraged*). Oh, all right. Have it your way.

LES. You little bum!

WANDA (*hurt and angry*). You lie! Hogan never touched me!

LES. Oh, no. And I suppose he didn't even try – that he had nothing but a wish to assist the poor little 'nigger gal' home?

WANDA. Am I responsible for what a man thinks?

LES. Phumn! Just as I thought. (*He turns away.*)

WANDA. We've got to have some place to stay, haven't we? Can't you see, Les? I only thought I might be able to borrow a few dollars from him!

LES. And you got them, I suppose?

WANDA. That's my business!

LES. You dirty little whore!

WANDA. Les!

LES. Any girl that'd stoop to such a thing and call herself decent –

WANDA. That's right! Wipe your feet on me! Drag me in the dirt!

LES. Ssh! Mama'll hear!

WANDA. Let her. I don't care! I don't care about nothing! (*She starts for front door*.)

LES (*catching her*). Keep your voice down!

WANDA (*twisting away from him*). I won't. You can tell the whole damn world for all I care. You think I'm nothing but a whore – why shouldn't she?

ELLA (*appearing from rear*). For God's sake, what's going on in here?

LES. Nothing, Mama.

WANDA. Oh, yes there is. Come on in. You'll get the thrill of your life. Les's got a little story to tell you – (*Turning to him, and going*.) Go on, Les, Tell her. Tell it to Mama. Give her your spicy little tale –

She runs into the street.

ELLA. What in the world is it?

LES. Nothing.

ELLA. Don't lie to me. What is it?

LES. She's just hysterical.

ELLA. Hysterical? Hysterical about what?

LES. The house, I guess. She's worried about the notice.

ELLA. You're lying. Tell me the truth!

LES. I am, Mama – she's worried about getting money for another place.

ELLA. What about this spicy tale business?

LES (*suddenly seeing a way out*). She came up with a wild
    scheme to raise money to get a place.

ELLA. What sort of wild scheme?

LES. It's unimportant, Mama. I've already put my foot down.
    Anyway, listen, I think we're going to get relief in another
    week or so.

ELLA (*puzzled*). What do you mean, 'relief'?

LES. Help, Mama – food, rent, maybe even employment.
    We're moving in on Governor Emerson tomorrow.

ELLA. Who's 'we'?

LES. Oh, just a bunch of folks like me, who're sick of waiting
    for 'prosperity to turn the corner'.

    DAN *re-enters.*

ELLA. And you're going with them,

LES. You bet!

DAN (*coming down*). Going where?

LES. To Springfield – to see the Governor about conditions.

ELLA. Have you said anything to your father?

LES. No. Not yet.

DAN. I guess not. You haven't forgotten what the police did to
    that mob in Ohio the other day, have you?

LES. I'm not worrying about that.

DAN. No. You and that bunch of riff-raff I see you with don't
    give a damn about nothing. But I warn you, you're headed
    for trouble!

LES. We're already in trouble. But you wouldn't understand
    that.

DAN. Well, there's one thing I do understand, and so will you
    reds before long!

LES (*laughing*). Yeah? What's that?

DAN. You can't beat the Government.

LES. You and your blind pessimism. You make me sick!

DAN. You'll learn when the rifles begin to talk!

LES. Let them. The quicker the better.

ELLA. Lester!

DAN. You young fool!

LES (*recklessly*). The disinherited will never come to power without bloodshed!

ELLA. Les! Don't say such things!

DAN. Let him rave on. He'll wake up one of these days.

LES (*seriously*). It's you who're asleep. Your world has crashed. But you're so full of capitalist dope, you don't even know we're building a new one.

He goes towards the kitchen.

DAN. You're building a wall to be put up against and shot!

LES (*going*). I'd rather look forward to that than a pauper's grave!

He exits.

ELLA. I don't know what in the world's come over him!

DAN. That's what you get for letting him raise himself!

ELLA. Don't blame me. I've done the best I could by him.

DAN. Yeah? For ten years all you and Vic've done is sit around here like a pair of petrified mummies and let him go straight to the dogs!

PERCY *is heard from the porch, singing drunkenly.*

PERCY.

'Is there anybody here want to buy a lil dog,
Buy a lil dog –

Appearing, he sways in doorway.

I got one to sell him . . . !'

LES *appears*.

DAN. Just look at that!

LES. Lay off him, Uncle Dan. (*Taking in the drunken man.*) Come on in, Uncle Percy, and sit down before you fall.

DAN. A regular bum!

Staggering, PERCY *pulls loose from* LES *and halts, swaying.*

PERCY. What do you mean, I'm a bum? Whatcha mean?

DAN. You'd better sit down and try to sober up!

PERCY (*fumbling in back pocket*). Sober up? Do I look like I'm drunk to you? Do I?

ELLA. You'd better take him in back and put him in Mama's room. He may get sick here.

LES. Come on, Uncle Percy. I'll put you to bed.

VIC *appears in doorway.* DAN *sees* PERCY *pulling a flask and tries to take it away.*

DAN. Gimme that!

PERCY (*hugging flask*). Oh no you don't, big shot. This is my moon.

VIC. Let him alone, Dan.

DAN (*angrily*). Can't you see he's drunk?

VIC *comes in, wearing his old Garvey uniform, which is now faded and bedraggled.*

VIC. What difference does it make!

PHILLIP *follows him in.*

PERCY (*triumphantly*). That a boy, Vic, old man. Get him told!

VIC (*to* LES, *quickly*). Take him somewhere and put him to bed. Go on now, Percy. Let him put you to bed.

PERCY. Awright, Vic. Anything you say, old man.

He allows LES *to escort him across to door leading to rear, where he halts.*

I know you wouldn't tell me nothing wrong – I know I must be drunk if you say so.

A ragged, broken, pathetic figure with one foot in the grave, he exits with LES.

DAN. He's going to keep on fighting that stuff until it kills him.

VIC. Maybe he'll be better off dead.

DAN. I judge you didn't come out so well . . . ?

VIC *avoids any direct contact with* ELLA, *with whom there has been no reconciliation and to whom he never speaks directly.*

VIC. No, I didn't.

DAN (*sympathetically*). How much time did the judge give you?

LES *re-enters.*

VIC (*hollowly*). Twenty days.

ELLA (*gasping*). Twenty days!

DAN (*astonished*). That all – ?

PHILLIP. I guess Papa was lucky to get that – (*Indicating his father's clothing.*) after the judge noticed the uniform.

VIC. He got tough when I admitted I used to be a Garveyite.

LES. What did he say, Papa?

VIC (*quoting, bitterly*). 'Oh, so you're one of the niggers who thinks this country isn't good enough for you, eh? Well, well, and you've got the nerve to appeal to this court for leniency?' As if that wasn't enough, he went on to rub it in telling me how thankful we ought to be because his people brought us out of savagery.

DAN (*after a moment*). Have you any idea what you're going to do?

VIC. Move to Hooverville, I guess.

DAN. Don't be sardonic, Vic.

VIC. If you think I don't mean it, find me a truck!

LES. Forget it, Papa. We're not going anywhere.

VIC. Eh?

LES. I said we're not going to move a step!

VIC. What're you talking about –

He stiffens, hearing MARTHA *on the porch.*

MARTHA (*calling*). Les! . . . Where's Les?

LES (*going to door, surprised*). It's Grandma!

The others sit amazed as MARTHA *enters in a huff, with a bundle of clothing under her arm.*

MARTHA. Les, I want you to go to Juanita's and bring me the rest of mah things. Cause I ain't fixin' to stay there another blessed night! (*Wearily, she drops into chair, centre.*)

ELLA. For God's sake, Mama – what's happened?

MARTHA. That hussy done forgot her raisin', dat's what! But if she thinks I'm goin' live in sich dirt, she never was so wrong in her life! Mah garment's clean and stainless 'fore the Saviour, and she and nobody else ain't goin' change it!

ELLA (*to* DAN). What in the world's she talking about?

DAN (*evasively*). Search me. It sounds like she's losing her mind.

MARTHA (*angrily*). Don't you try to call me crazy, you sneakin' blackguard! If you don't want me to lay you out, don't you open your mouth!

DAN. Aw, go on, Mama – whatever it is, forget it! Ella and Vic don't want to hear that stuff. They've got trouble enough of their own –

ELLA (*suspicious of him*). Never mind about that, Dan. Go on. Mama. What is it?

MARTHA (*to* DAN). You needn't think you can shut me up, neither! 'Cause –

DAN. Shut you up! Why should I want to shut you up? (*Turning to others and quickly crossing to window.*) If you all want to listen to her crazy tales, let her go ahead, it doesn't make a damn bit of difference to me what she says!

ELLA. Go on, Mama. What happened?

MARTHA. I got after her 'bout rentin' rooms and havin' all kinds of lowdown, good-for-nothin' tramps layin' up in her house – (*Glancing around at* DAN.) while some folks I ain't mentionin' keep duckin' in and out and and makin' out they can't see what's goin' on. So she says: 'Mama, do you know how you're livin'? Do you know who's takin' care of you? Do you know nobody's givin' me a dime to look after this house? Where you think I'm goin' git rent to keep a roof ovuh your head?' As if I never kept a roof ovah bofe of you heads for twenty years without degradin' maself – But ask me if I didn't curse her out? I bet you she'll remember what I told her to her dyin' day! – After that, I just got mah things together and come on to you, 'cause I know you'd give me a clean place to lay mah weary head, even if we did fall out 'bout the chillun and Vic and me had a word or two – 'cause I know he ain't goin' hold no more malice against me for what I said 'bout him, than I hold against him for what he said 'bout me –

She turns to her son-in-law.

Now ain't that right, Vic?

VIC (*smiling, admiring her shrewdness*). Of course, Mama. (*His smile fading.*) Though I'm sorry to say things ain't like they used to be here. We're just about to be kicked into the street, and if something don't happen in the next twenty days, we will be. But you're welcome to stay if you want to.

MARTHA. Twenty days!

ELLA. Twenty days!

MARTHA. Lawd, Lawd.

She catches sight of DAN *smiling gloatingly.*

But I'd head rather sleep in the street with you all than stain mah garment in the wallow they got ovah there!

LES. Don't worry, Grandma. A lot can happen in twenty days!

Curtain.

Scene Two

Three weeks later.

The light of a small lamp is burning, revealing the room in upheaval. There are packing cases and barrels about, showing that the family is preparing to vacate the premises, or to be evicted.

Though it is nearly 3.30 a.m., MARTHA, *in an old, frazzle-edged robe, is seen alone, peering out into the night from the window. In a moment, she turns towards the door, expectantly, as* LES *enters.*

MARTHA (*her voice hushed but excited*). Les, has you seen anything of Wanda?

LES (*arrested*). Wanda? – No. Why do you ask?

MARTHA (*sotto voce*). She ain't come in this house yet – and it's after three o'clock.

LES (*placing batch of leaflets on table*). Wanda's a grown woman, Grandma.

MARTHA. Grown or not grown, she's got no business out in the streets this time o' night – I'm worried 'bout her.

LES. You'd better go back to bed and try to get some sleep. (*Laughing, as he turns to climb stairs.*) You may not get another chance after tonight, you know!

MARTHA (*arresting him*). I ain't worried 'bout that. But somethin' musta happened to Wanda!

LES (*joining her to give her a pat*). You're just imagining things, Grandma. Go on back to bed.

MARTHA (*tightening her robe*). I can't sleep – how Ella can, beats me. After the way she cried round here these last few days – 'specially this afternoon 'fore Wanda come. Then she got calm as a picture of a saint . . . (*Probingly.*) You reckon Wanda coulda told her somethin'?

LES. Now, Grandma, what do you suppose she could've told her?

MARTHA. I dunno. Neither one of them don't talk to me like they used to. (*Going back to window*.) You'd think I was some stranger round here.

LES. Oh, they're just worried – just as you are. (*Going*.) But I'm going to bed. Goodnight!

MARTHA (*peering out of window*). Wait, Les! (*Waving to him, excitedly*.) Come here a minute and see if that ain't Claudine yonder!

LES (*joining her*). Claudine! . . . (*He sees figure*.) Now what do you know about that? It's her all right –

He goes to the door to open it and call in a whispered voice:

Claudine! Come here!

MARTHA. I told you there was somethin' wrong. I knowed it. My mind don't fool me!

LES (*as the girl approaches*). Claudine, what in the world are you doing out in the street this time of night?

CLAUDINE *appears. She is wearing a gown with a lace stole around her shoulders.*

CLAUDINE (*anxiously*). Wanda here?

LES (*closing door behind her*). No.

CLAUDINE. She ain't come home?

LES. No, not yet – why? There isn't anything wrong, is there?

CLAUDINE. No. I just wanted to see her.

MARTHA. It's mighty funny you got to be watchin' for her in the street, instid of coming to this house!

LES. Claudine, you're hiding something –

CLAUDINE. No, really – Wanda's all right. (*Going*.) You'll see if she isn't – I was just –

MARTHA (*intercepting her*). You hold on!

LES. No, Grandma! For God's sake! Leave it to me.

MARTHA. How come I can't be trusted?

LES. It isn't that, Grandma. You wait here –

He starts out with CLAUDINE.

MARTHA (*striding to stairs*). Maybe she'll talk to Ella.

LES (*whirling to grab her*). No, Grandma!

He sees CLAUDINE *is escaping.*

Wait Claudine! Wait! (*Desperately.*) For God's sake, keep your mouth shut until I get back.

He runs out, leaving the door open in his haste to catch the fleeing girl. MARTHA *rushes to the window to remain there in her frustration, staring into the darkened street.*

Blackout.

Scene Three

Several hours later.

ELLA *is packing blankets into a case.*

ELLA (*calling into kitchen*). Caroline, haven't you finished with those dishes yet?

CAROLINE (*offstage*). Oh, give me time, Mama. I'll be through in a minute!

ELLA. You've been at them long enough to have them washed and packed too. Lord, if I don't lose my mind this morning, I never will!

CAROLINE (*entering with armful of plates*). Well, it's not doing you any good to worry. Wanda and Les are both probably together somewhere.

She goes to barrel and begins packing dishes.

ELLA. It's mighty funny neither your father nor Phillip's been able to find them.

CAROLINE. You'd do better worrying about what we're going to do when the bailiffs come.

ELLA. We ain't going to do nothing but let them set us out. Then I'm going to thank them for doing us a favour.

CAROLINE. What?

ELLA (*turning with a smile*). I've got the money, Caroline, to get a place!

CAROLINE. You have?

ELLA. Yes. Wanda gave me $50 yesterday!

CAROLINE. Mama, you're joking?

ELLA (*pulling a roll of bills from her bosom and waving them triumphantly*). What do you call this?

CAROLINE. Where'd she get all that money?

ELLA (*laughing with joy*). Her boss. He loaned it to her.

VIC (*appearing in open door*). Well, did she get back?

CAROLINE. No. Didn't you find her?

VIC (*coming in, wearily*). No. Nobody's seen hide nor hair of her. And she hasn't been near the drugstore since early last night.

CAROLINE. What about Les – was there no trace of him?

VIC (*shaking his head negatively*). I went to the reds and saw Piszer. But he said Les left the park about 2.30 this morning, on his way here.

CAROLINE. Well, he never showed up. His bed hasn't been slept in.

ELLA. Lord, I wish that telephone wasn't disconnected!

VIC *averts his eyes in the manner he has for several years now, whenever he addresses a remark for his wife's benefit.*

VIC. I already called the police, and every hospital in town.

MARTHA (*entering with old suitcase, and seeing* VIC). Where's she?

VIC. I've had no luck.

CAROLINE (*seeing* WANDA *and* LES *in door*). Here they are!

VIC. Thank God!

ELLA. Where've you been?

WANDA (*lying*). I'm sorry, Mama. But I was in an accident. Claudine and I went for a ride to Gary with some fellows last night, and the car broke down.

MARTHA. Claudine and you! Then what was she doing here lookin' for you at three o'clock this mornin'?

ELLA (*surprised*). Three o'clock this morning!

LES (*covering for* WANDA). You don't understand, Grandma. The car Wanda was in broke down, and Claudine and them, not knowing it, came on. But when they got here and the rest didn't show up, naturally, Claudine was afraid something might've happened to her.

MARTHA (*sighing*). Oh, well.

WANDA. I thought several times we were going to have to walk back.

ELLA (*relieved, but motherly*). It would've served you right! Worrying everybody to death!

WANDA (*going*). I'm sorry, Mama. But it couldn't be helped. I'm going up and wash.

She exits above.

VIC. Well, this sure is a relief. (*Taking seat.*) Now if only the bailiffs weren't due, I'd feel like celebrating.

CAROLINE. Shucks, Papa. Who cares about the bailiffs? They're welcome to set us out, aren't they, Mama?

ELLA (*proudly, as she continues packing*). I reckon they can come if they want to.

VIC (*to* CAROLINE). What're you talking about? You think it's a joke to have to sleep in the park?

CAROLINE. Papa, Mama's got the money to rent us a new place!

MARTHA. What's that?

CAROLINE. Wanda borrowed it from her boss yesterday.

VIC. God be praised!

LES. Forget it, Papa. This is no matter for rejoicing.

VIC. Why not?

LES. You can't afford to take this way out.

ELLA *is puzzled, her heart skipping a beat.*

VIC. I don't think I understand you, Les.

MARTHA. Sounds like he's crazy.

LES. You've a duty to others, Papa.

VIC. What duty?

PISZER (*entering open door*). Good morning, folks!

LES. To yourself and thousands facing eviction this morning –
    (*Ironically*.) with no daughter lucky enough to borrow from
    her boss!

VIC. You mean, refuse to get out?

LES. It's the only way to stop the landlords, Papa.

VIC. You're asking me to turn the family into guineapigs, son.

LES. Our only hope is in resistance. You saw what good it did
    us trying to appeal to the Governor, didn't you?

VIC. Lester. A poor Negro like me can only get it in the neck
    if he bucks the law – and anything may happen in another
    month.

LES *is desperate, knowing he cannot use the knowledge he
    possesses without disloyalty to* WANDA.

LES. In another month you'll be right back where you started
    from! Suppose you take the money Mama's got and rent
    another place? Can Wanda keep up the rent? Do you think
    her boss is going to play the sweet angel again?

PISZER. We put ten families back in their homes this week.
    We can do the same for you, Mr Mason. Say the word
    and in ten minutes we'll have a thousand comrades at your
    door –

JUANITA *rushes in with* DAN *at her heels*.

JUANITA. Has she come yet, Ella?

ELLA. Yes. She's upstairs. She and Claudine drove off to Gary
    with some young men and the car broke down. But they got
    back all right.

JUANITA. Well, I'm sure glad to hear that. I was worried to death.

DAN. Me too! (*Jovially, to* VIC.) Well, old man, see you're still here.

VIC. Yeah. But my time ain't long.

DAN. Well, don't let it worry you. You all can come over to my house, though I can't promise you how long it'll be before they kick us out.

VIC. Thanks very much, Dan. But – (*He glances uneasily at* LES.) we've got the money for a place.

JUANITA. You have – ?

CAROLINE. Yes. Wanda borrowed it from her boss yester –

PHILLIP (*bursting in to blurt*). Papa, you know what? Wanda's in jail!

VIC (*laughing*). In jail! Why, you're crazy –

The others join in the laughter, believing it's a good joke.

PHILLIP (*defensively*). Well, Claudine said so!

ELLA. She did?

PHILLIP. Yes she did! She told me –

LES (*interposes*). Aw, you don't know what you're talking about. Wanda and Claudine both spent the night in Gary. She's upstairs now!

PHILLIP. She is?

LES. Sure.

PHILLIP. Then why did Claudine go telling me that stuff for – ?

ELLA (*still suspicious*). What did she say?

LES (*interposing, as he glares at* PHILLIP). Don't pay any attention to him, Mama. Claudine's just been pulling his leg.

PHILLIP. Pulling nothing! How you know she wasn't in jail? How you know she didn't just get out on bond, like Claudine said she would.

ELLA. Claudine said that?

LES. But Mama, I tell you –

ELLA. You shut up! And let me hear the rest of this. Go on, Phillip, what did she say?

PHILLIP (*aware at last that something is wrong, but unable to restrain himself*). She said Wanda got caught in a raid last night –

JUANITA. A raid?

PHILLIP. With some white man named Hogan. But for us not to worry because the woman who runs the place was going to get her out on bond this morning.

The family is stunned.

MARTHA (*outraged*). Caught in a raid with a white man! I knowed it! I knowed it! I warned you, Ella. I –

LES. For God's sakes, Grandma, hush your mouth.

MARTHA. Don't you tell me to hush!

PHILLIP. Claudine said they'd have caught her too, if she hadn't run for it.

ELLA (*striding to foot of stairs, and calling, imperiously*). Wanda! You come down here to me!

VIC. I can't believe Wanda's mixed up in anything like this.

ELLA (*as WANDA appears above*). Come down here!

JUANITA. Give her a chance, Ella!

ELLA (*coldly*). Where were you last night?

WANDA. I – I just told you. Me and Claudine –

ELLA. I want the truth!

WANDA. I'm telling you, Mama!

ELLA. Didn't you just get out of jail?

WANDA. No, no – Who said that? (*To LES accusingly*.) Les – (*She catches herself.*)

ELLA (*shooting in the dark*). Oh, so you were!

Striding to LES, WANDA strikes him across the mouth. LES turns away and all are silent in their pain.

JUANITA. Lord have mercy, Wanda. He didn't do it. It was Phillip.

WANDA. Phillip?

JUANITA. Yes.

WANDA (*quietly*). I'm sorry, Les.

LES. Forget it.

ELLA. Is it true, too, you were laying up with a white man?

WANDA (*on the verge of tears*). You had to have the money, Mama –

Pathetically, her eyes search their faces for a sign of understanding.

What else could I do?

Unable to face their stony silence, she lingers for a moment, then runs above to hide her shame. ELLA *turns to the window with bowed head.*

MARTHA (*dumbfounded*). Lawd, Lawd, Lawd!

LES (*to* PHILLIP). I guess you're satisfied.

PHILLIP *turns away.*

VIC. Well, I reckon this changes the face of everything. (*To* LES, *ready at last to fight.*) Suppose you can still get help?

LES. All you want, Papa.

DAN. The reds?

VIC (*firmly*). Get them. The bailiffs'll be along any minute.

LES (*going*). Come on, Piszer!

They exit, running.

JUANITA. You're making an awful mistake, Vic!

VIC. I've got to stand my ground!

DAN. But there'll be trouble, man!

VIC (*bitterly*). I got a taste for trouble now!

JUANITA. Oh, Vic, why be a fool?

VIC. I suppose you think I should use that tainted money!

ELLA *whirls*.

JUANITA. I thought she borrowed it!

VIC. We all fools to think so – the little tramp!

ELLA – *outraged, her old animosity surging up to condemn him – extracts the roll of money and hurls it into face.*

ELLA. Here! You take this! It belongs to you!

DAN. Ella!

JUANITA (*stepping between them*). Oh, Ella – for heaven's sake!

ELLA (*as* VIC *stands bewildered*). Get out of my way, and don't tell me nothing!

CAROLINE. Mama, Mama, please!

PERCY *enters, half-drunk and unshaven.*

ELLA (*raging*). Calling somebody a tramp! Who made her a tramp?

JUANITA. Don't, Ella!

ELLA (*storming*). Who started her on the road to hell?

DAN. Ella!

ELLA. With something less than a black fool for a father she was booked for the gutter!

VIC (*bowed beneath the impact as one before a fatal blow*). Yeah . . .

PERCY *sobers*.

JUANITA. Oh, Ella. How can you say such a cruel thing?

ELLA. You ask me how? I'll tell you how. Because I'm sick to death of him, that's how! I thought I had enough when he talked like he did to Mama. But now that I've lived to see my child ruined on account of his stupidity, there's nothing I'd like better than to see him dead!

PERCY (*angrily, to* VIC). You going to stand there and let her talk to you like that?

VIC. That's all right, Ella. It's all right –

BAILIFF (*appearing in door with* MEN *behind him*). Does Victor Mason live here?

DAN. Yes. What is it?

BAILIFF (*entering, followed by his* MEN). I've a court order to evict you. (*To his men.*) Come on, boys. Get to work!

Without further ado, the MEN *begin removing furnishings.*

VIC (*deadly serious*). You can save yourselves a lot of trouble, if you let that stuff alone!

BAILIFF (*as* MEN *pause*). What d'you mean?

VIC. I'm not going to stand no eviction!

BAILIFF. Are you looking for trouble?

VIC. Call it what you like –

He halts, hearing voices chanting as they approach in the distance.

PHILLIP (*at window*). It's Les and them. A whole army of them!

BAILIFF. The reds. (*To* VIC.) Well, you'd better call them off! They won't get away with *this* case?!

Police sirens roar in the distance.

DAN (*frightened*). Vic, my offer still stands!

VIC. And what're you going to do when they set *you* out?

DAN. There'll be time enough to think of that later.

The sirens cease, as brakes are heard screeching.

BAILIFF (*to his* MEN). Go on, boys. Set 'em out!

As MEN *carry out pieces, he turns to* VIC, *warningly.*

You'd better be reasonable! The cops have their orders! We're not going to stand for any more interference!

VIC strides to door. PHILLIP *attempts to follow him.*

VIC (*to* PHILLIP). Go back!

BAILIFF (*following to door, as* VIC *disappears outside*). All right. You're asking for it!

MARTHA (*in terror*). Have mercy, Jesus!

The sound of the chanting increases, then is suddenly drowned out by the screech of another siren, and silence reigns.

PISZER (*commandingly, outside*). All right, comrades. Let's go!

CAROLINE (*at window*). They're bringing the things back!

LIEUTENANT (*ominously, outside*). Halt! In the name of the law I order you not to interfere!

VOICES, *rising, chant again.*

LIEUTENANT. Halt! Halt! I order you to halt!

MARTHA. Help us, sweet Jesus!

VIC *is seen on the porch at head-end of piece of furniture. There is the sudden roar of gunfire, and* VIC *is seen clutching the door jamb. Another of his companions is seen to fall.*

VIC (*groaning*). Ahhhhhah!

He clings to the door jamb, where shortly he is caught by LES. DAN *runs to join them.*

LES. Help me get him to the couch –

CAROLINE *attempts to assist.*

Move, Caroline!

WANDA (*appearing above, appalled by the sight of her father*). Oh God!

She runs below, as LES *and* DAN *succeed in placing* VIC *on couch.*

VOICE (*offstage*). They've shot two of them!

PERCY (*suddenly enraged, rushing to doorway in a futile gesture of defiance*). You goddamn murdering bastards! You dirty killers!

DAN *runs up to grab him and pull him inside.*

Turn me loose, Dan. Turn me loose!

DAN (*wrestling him into chair*). No, Percy! No!

PERCY (*in tears, his stupor gone*). Bastards shot my brother!

LES. Shot in the back, like a dog!

LIEUTENANT *appears with a* PATROLMAN.

LIEUTENANT (*turns to call over his shoulder*). Yeah. There's one in here! (*Coming down.*) Who told you to move that man?

PERCY (*springing up*). Get the hell out of here!

DAN *grabs him.*

Don't, Dan.

WANDA (*joining them*). Please, Uncle Percy.

LIEUTENANT (*to* LES). I asked you who gave you orders to move that man?

LES (*bitterly*). What are we supposed to do, let him lie there like a dog?

LIEUTENANT (*looking around*). You shouldn't've moved him! (*To* PATROLMAN.) Get an ambulance.

PATROLMAN. They've already sent in the call.

LES. How do you feel, Papa?

VIC. Just kind of numb.

LES *casts an appealing glance to his mother, but she turns to the window.*

The BAILIFFS *are re-entering, but the doorway fills at once with grim-faced white and black men, acting in concert to prevent any further removal of furnishings.*

LIEUTENANT. Get back! Clear out of here!

The workers are immobile, and he pulls his gun.

I said clear out of here!

PISZER. We're not budging!

PATROLMAN (*after a moment*). I think we'd better call in, Lieutenant. These bastard're crazy.

LIEUTENANT (*to* BAILIFFS). You fellows had better drop this until we get further orders. (*Going.*) Let us by!

The MEN *in the doorway, accepting the victory, fall back, and the* LIEUTENANT *exits, the* BAILIFFS *following.*

VIC (*weakly*). Where's Ella?

LES (*glances toward her, but she doesn't turn, and he lies*). She went in the back for a minute, Papa.

VIC. Don't lie, son. (*Shortly.*) Lift my head up.

CAROLINE *drops to her knees beside him.* LES *raises pillow, and turns toward his mother.*

LES. Mama . . . ! Please!

VIC. Don't, son. I reckon she's got cause enough to hate me.

He pauses to gather his strength. He caresses CAROLINE'*s hair.*

I want you to stick by each other and never let nothing come between you. (*Turning to* WANDA.) And that goes for you, too, Wanda.

She bows her head in silence.

I spoke a little hard about you . . . But I didn't mean it . . . because I understand. (*After a moment.*) You'll all find it pretty hard . . . like Les said . . . 'This world ain't . . . nothing but . . . big white . . . '

LES (*quietly*). I was mistaken, Papa.

VIC. You think so?

LES. I know I was. But you be quiet now, and don't tax your strength.

VIC. I've got to talk, son.

WANDA. Oh, God!

CAROLINE. No, Papa –

VIC. Go on, Les.

LES. Only, that I was looking in the wrong direction, Papa.

VIC. Yes?

LES. There is light.

VIC. What light?

LES. Look in the door, Papa.

LES searches within for the means to express his truth. Then turns to the door with its crowded faces.

VIC *(straining upward)*. What is it? . . . I can't seem to see.

LES. It's my comrades –

VIC. Your comrades – ?

LES. Yes. You remember?

VIC. Yes, of course – I owe them –

LES. It's not that, Papa. I wanted you to see them – black and white.

VIC. Where are they?

PISZER *(quietly)*. Here.

VIC. I guess my sight is gone. *(He sinks back.)*

CAROLINE. Papa!

WANDA. Don't go, Papa! Come back, come back!

LES *(examining him)*. He's gone!

He turns away, broken. ELLA, hearing his verdict, turns from the window.

ELLA, relenting, creeps toward the dead man, her voice filled with grief.

ELLA *(scarcely audible)*. Vic! . . . Vic!

In the distance an ambulance siren is heard, and slowly the curtain descends.